ALIGN
&
SHINE

First printing: 2022
ISBN-13: 978-0-9956849-5-9

Published by Butterfly House Publishing
Cover design by Marianne Hartley

British Cataloguing Publication Data: A catalogue record of this book is available from The British Library.

ALIGN
&
SHINE

Gain an unshakable foundation
to build your legacy brand

MARIANNE HARTLEY

'There's not a lot that you can call genuinely magical. Most magic turns out to be a trick or an entertaining deception – the more you know, the less impressive it is. The most genuinely magical thing I have ever witnessed is what happens when you get into alignment. Alignment starts with yourself, doing things that you feel completely on purpose for. Then it spreads; other people align to the vision and the mission and then the magic starts. Great products, memorable brands, winning teams, high-performing campaigns all start coming in thick and fast once that alignment happens. You can see when people, teams, businesses and brands are in alignment – they shine brightly. Marianne has captured this idea in her book and sheds light on the awesome power of being up to something. Alignment isn't a magic trick, it's genuine and there's a process for making it happen in this book.'

Daniel Priestley Founder of Dent Global, author of *Key Person of Influence*

'This is a great book and a far cry from the usual business books. I felt I was drawn into a conversation and the client stories drew me in and helped me to reflect on how I feel about my own situation. The exercises at the end of each chapter are really great.'

Alison Kriel Founder, Above & Beyond Education

'Marianne's expertise shines throughout this book. She took me on a guided journey full of key, interesting and timeless messages to establish a brand that is true to my purpose.'

Dr Kirren Brah Integrated Medical Practitioner and Academic

'I had planned to read a part of this book on a Sunday afternoon in the garden. Hours later and sitting in the same spot, I had read the whole thing! I was left feeling energised and empowered, sitting alongside lots of notes and ideas on my brand and business as a whole. I've been lucky enough to work with Marianne in the past, and reading this book was a fantastic reminder, fully cementing my previous learning with her. Although I have already designed my brand, working through the book helped me to develop that and my wider vision further.'
Sara Maxwell Founder, Wealth Coach

'This is an intelligent and inspirational guide to creating a brand that people can fall in love with. With enjoyable exercises and heartening examples, I would recommend it to any purpose-driven entrepreneur or business owner who wants to learn how to build a brand that can help them do the power of good.'
Natasha Wardle Spiritual Business Coach

'Read this book if you have a business or a brand that you are looking to take to the next level. Align & Shine is both a call to action and a road map for developing beautiful brands that will shine brightly for years to come.'
Ansal Trafford Proofreader and Copywriter

'You're thinking about branding in the new world – read this.'
Sue Ingram Founder of Converse Well, author of *Fire Well*

CONTENTS

FOREWORD

I knew from the moment I met Marianne that there was more to her branding approach than met the eye.

When I worked with her to create the Iconic Shift brand, this proved to be true. There are many designers and brand strategists, but few have the ability to draw out the essence of a person and business idea and translate it into a beautiful design that engages all your senses. This is a gift Marianne has. Having worked with large branding agencies to create the Firstdirect and Egg brands, this was a different perspective and a very new approach to the brand creation process.

We are at a point in history where people crave truthful, real and authentic connection with themselves, others and the world. This is reflected in what we buy, how we buy and from whom. More and more people buy from brands they trust, believe in and feel in alignment with.

Your best ally for being successful and staying successful is your brand. Unlike product features, your brand is really hard to copy. You reap the economic benefits, you attract the right people, you keep them, clients recommend you, they buy more from you, and the value that creates is enormous. The power of a brand is extraordinary.

Why is your brand such a differentiator and why is it so hard to copy? Because it is created from the inside out. It comes from the heart!

The second I saw the design Marianne created for the brand I thought, 'God, this reminds me instantly why I am doing this in the first place.' It got me an emotional reaction. And the only way to get an emotional reaction from design is if the design is beautiful. That generates a calmness and clarity, almost like meditation.

Working with Marianne Hartley from Hartley & Soul was a pleasure and delight. Having someone who not only understands you but also really gets what it is you want to create is priceless.

If you want to create a brand that is part of the solution to the many challenges our world faces today, then read this book, as Marianne guides you through the steps to connect the deepest part of your purpose to the highest outcome of your vision to turn it into an iconic brand.

Mike Harris
Founder, Iconic Shift
Firstdirect and Egg

INTRODUCTION
My Story: How I Came to Branding

I grew up in a small village in the French speaking part of Switzerland, surrounded by nature and cows. I spent most of my time outdoors, playing in the garden, exploring the nearby woodland and climbing trees. I just loved being perched on a branch, cradled by the tree, seeing a different perspective. Looking at the texture of the bark or the pattern of a leaf. I spent a lot of time looking at things in small detail and was in awe of the colours, shapes and patterns nature displays. To me, it was an infinitely fascinating and beautiful world.

When I was about five we got a TV, and the only things I wanted to watch – besides *Little House on The Prairie* – were the ads. I was mesmerised by them. The way ads were able to tell a story in such a short time captivated me.

One of my mum's dearest friends was an eccentric artist called Ida, with whom we spent many weekends visiting exhibitions in galleries and museums. We spent hours in these spaces and even though, as a small child, I often felt bored, there was one particular exhibition that had a big impact on me. This is when I realised the power of image. It was an exhibition in Bern by Swiss painter Ferdinand Hodler; a series of paintings of his partner at the end of her life. The paintings weren't happy. They were stark, tragic and looked very real – and they affected me.

This was in contrast to the atmosphere in the exhibition space, which was calm, beautiful and serene; something I didn't experience anywhere else. Even though I felt challenged by the subject of the paintings, the energy of the space was soothing and nourishing. I must have been seven years old when I saw this exhibition and the impact was so strong that I remember it to this day.

With a child's curiosity, I noticed that there weren't many people present at the exhibition compared to how many people were outside. I didn't understand why. Because to me, the stories I experienced and the connection I felt with the paintings were much more appealing than the images on billboards that I saw out on the street. It gave me a very different experience even though the medium was similar: a picture in a frame.

In the gallery, each painting was an invitation that drew me in to question, reflect and connect and left me feeling enriched, expanded and nourished. The billboard images I saw were the opposite: they seemed to be leaping out at me, they were loud, and they left me feeling like I'd been punched in the face. They were highly visible and impossible to miss but they were brash and one-dimensional. They lacked depth and weren't particularly beautiful. It made me question why there was such a huge difference between the two and, much later, whether there had to be.

The challenge of good branding is not only to have clarity and convey a single message, but also to invoke the depth of connection and nuances like a work of art does. It's seeing the branding once and feeling like it is talking to you and that you know it. It conveys something beautiful; you experience an emotional reaction and feel enriched and nourished by it, and you want to experience more.

As a teenager, I noticed that most advertising didn't make me feel very good. The images I saw suggested I needed to look a certain way or have certain things in order to fit into an image of what happiness looks like. I now understand this to be consumerism and manipulation through creating a sense of lack. I question, in our current throwaway society with climate change and rampant consumerism, why this still is the purpose of branding and advertising.

Consumerism is destroying our planet *and* our emotional and mental wellbeing. Buying more products doesn't lead to happiness like advertising implies, nor does it fill the inner void we experience or remove the sense of not being good enough that we all experience at times. Instead, it leads to a greater sense of disconnection from ourselves, a feeling of isolation that makes us feel that 'something must be wrong with me'.

I was left wondering why we couldn't bring the beautiful energy and connection I experienced with art in galleries out into the world for more people to see, feel and benefit from.

Wouldn't it be great if the images we saw on a daily basis made us feel *really* good and reminded us of who we are, why we are here and what we are here to do?

This became my driving force for studying graphic design.

After completing a 5-year degree at l'Ecole d'Art Appliqués in La Chaux-de-Fonds, Switzerland – where Le Corbusier studied, many moons before – I arrived in London with my portfolio under my arm and a list of design agencies I wanted to work for.

I freelanced for various design companies and worked on a broad spectrum of projects, ranging from international hotels to global insurance companies, where I learned about brand positioning, brand hierarchy and strategy. I loved the work but felt there was a dimension missing. My interest in the mind-body-spirit connection led me to study energy healing and Buddhism.

It opened up a whole new world that I was fascinated by and keen to combine with my love of creating beautiful designs. This led to creating Hartley & Soul many years later, to clearly communicate a product or service to buyers, whilst at the same time designing an image of beauty that uplifts the viewer and connects to the heart.

My intention with this book

As you are holding this book in your hands, you are probably at one of three places:

1. You've just had a business idea and you want to turn it into a brand, but you have no idea how to go about it.

2. You've been running a successful business for some time and you love what you do, but you've outgrown your current brand as it no longer reflects who you are and this is holding you back. You know there is something missing because you are no longer attracting the clients you wish to work with, but you don't know what that is.

3. You're a serial entrepreneur and have set up successful businesses in the past, but this time you are looking to bring the biggest version of yourself and your business into the world and you need a co-vision holder to create an iconic brand with you.

Whichever stage you find yourself at, you're in the right place.

This book is here to equip you with the invisible aspects you need to build an unshakable foundation for your brand, and brief a design agency or designer to translate it into your visual brand identity.

The process will engage every aspect of you to create balance and alignment by accessing both sides of the brain to create a brand that embodies both logic and intuition, so it is grounded and practical yet aspirational.

My dream is to see visionary business owners with beautiful brands that are a true reflection of their values making an impact in the world. As a result, attracting their ideal clients and employees becomes easier, more effortless and more fun too.

My intention with this book is to lift your spirit and inspire you. So you can create a brand that is in true alignment with who you are so that you can do what you came here to do with ease, joy and satisfaction.

Before creating the design of your brand, there are three key stages that will ensure you have a solid foundation from which to build it:

1. Dive
2. Discover
3. Define

Dive is about diving deep and seeing what lies under the surface. It is about digging the foundation, removing what is in the way, highlighting what is unique and drawing out what it is you are here to contribute: who you are being, the problem you are here to solve and for whom.

This first stage is linked to the left brain, the logical side, and all questions act as pointers to help us unearth what you and your brand stand for.

The second stage is **Discover**, which is about connecting with intuition, the right brain. Here, we engage with our heart to give us the next level of information: a deeper level of understanding that we wouldn't have access to with our logical side alone.

The third stage is **Define**, where we bring it all together, linking logic and intuition, left and right sides of our brain and our heart and soul to consolidate the foundations of a balanced, cohesive and coherent brand.

Imagine having a beautiful brand you feel proud of, that gives you confidence, that elevates you, that your clients love and recognise you by and that makes you feel in love with your business.

This is the power and promise of an aligned brand.

You will find an exercise at the end of every chapter. I suggest you choose a comfortable space, a beautiful notebook and your favourite pen to capture all your answers. Putting the principles of this book into practice will give you the solid foundation you need to take your business to the next level.

My wish for you is that you discover the unique beauty of your brand, so you can be authentically you and shine your light in the world.

Let's dive in!

PART 1: DIVE

DIVING IN | PLOUGHING THE FIELD |
UNEARTHING | DIGGING THE FOUNDATION

– Left Brain –

'If you want to go high, you need to go deep.'
Marianne Hartley

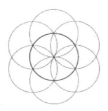

CHAPTER 1
What is Your WHY?

Client story

Four years ago, Francesca Cassini set up an online membership community, The Silver Tent, to create opportunities for women aged over 50 from all over the world to come together, connect and support each other. Her greatest vision is to see millions of women from different walks of life and cultures weaving together their unique skills, gifts, perceptions and understanding. In the centre of this will be Silver Philanthropy, which she sees as a thriving charitable enterprise serving a million women to bring their heartfelt projects to life, not just with financial support but also with expertise from the community to manifest their visions into the world. In its full glory, The Silver Tent will profoundly serve the global community with its untapped reservoir of the wisdom of women from around the world.

When she came to see me, The Silver Tent was a Facebook group with 7000 members. Francesca wanted to increase her reach with her own online presence but was feeling held back by not having a clear brand. During the one day brand alignment session we discovered that her legacy is to 'create paradigm shifts in human consciousness' and to 'rewrite the myth of the older woman'.

'I felt hampered by what I was able to offer people,'

Francesca said. 'Even though I had the vision firmly in my heart of what I wanted to create, it was as if it really was immaterial; it felt like a pipe dream.

'What I experienced with Marianne is that she got everything I shared about my vision for The Silver Tent. She understood it without me saying a lot. It's like energetically she understood it.

'When you have a brand that captures the heart and soul, it elevates your business and translates into this most beautiful space on the website and in our community. It's got a pristine feeling about it and such a beautiful high energy. It's quite something to know we co-created this together.'

I believe we all have unique gifts and talents that we are here to share and contribute to make the world a better place. You have something to bring to your field, industry or sector that no one else can do exactly the way you do.

The first thing to do when creating your brand is to fully connect with your vision and the WHY of your business and take a deep dive into your reason for doing what you are doing. This is the first step we go through in the brand alignment session.

The analogy I use to describe the process is like digging the foundation of a building and making sure it is deep enough to hold what we want to build, whether that's a chalet or a skyscraper.

It is also like ploughing a field: checking the quality of the soil, removing any big rocks and dead roots that are in the way and making sure the quality of the soil will enable the seeds we plant to grow strong roots for our brand to thrive in this terrain.

We need to dig deep to unearth the treasure, the uniqueness that you are here to share.

Whether you are creating your first or tenth brand, discovering your WHY is all about asking yourself the right questions.

Knowing what your WHY is, defining it and owning it is a fundamental aspect of your brand and will become the anchor of your brand's solid foundation.

It is likely to result in what you will be known for to your audience and very likely to become the legacy you leave behind.

Whether you are creating a local business serving your community or a global brand serving millions of people around the world, your WHY will be bigger than just you and your business.

It is the drive, the purpose, the reason beyond money for which your business is a conduit through which you play your most empowering and satisfying game.

Your WHY may have been with you in your heart since childhood or it might have emerged through a recent challenge or by seeing something missing in your field of expertise.

Whether it has been with you for a long time or just recently came to you, claiming it and owning it will not only inspire you to do the work you love. It will also inspire others who feel aligned with your vision to join you and help you make it a reality and buy from you.

Many businesses focus their attention on the financial outcome they want to achieve with the company, often forgetting to put an equal focus on how they are feeling and *being* while achieving this goal. Although many businesses are now realising the power of ensuring their employees feel an integral part of bringing their vision to life, there are still too many who don't. When they choose not to engage the hearts of their employees this can lead to lower levels of engagement, a lack of resourcefulness, stress and feelings of disconnection. Why? Because the business is driven by an idea and employees are asked to do just a job rather than being an integral part of helping an organisation bring their vision to life.

This reminds me of the beautiful story of a man who was sweeping the office building at NASA. When President John F Kennedy visited in 1962, he asked the man what he was doing. The man answered, broom in hand: 'I'm helping put a man on the moon.'

This is a brilliant example of an employee feeling part of the vision, no matter what role they play in the company. When this level of connection is present within organisations, magic happens.

Which makes you feel more motivated: going to work to earn money, or playing a part in bringing an organisation's vision to life?

Impactful brands are driven by a powerful vision that attracts talent into the organisation, people who resonate with it and want to play their part in bringing the vision to life. They are not driven by financial goals alone.

Powerful brands engage our heads and our hearts; they stimulate both the logical and intuitive sides of our brains.

Every influential brand is clear on its why, its "raison d'être", its "reason for being".

It is the heart and soul, the core, the essence of the creation of your brand.

Without it, your brand is like a house of cards, a boat without a compass or a label on an empty jar.

With it, you have an unshakable foundation and your North Star, your navigation map for your brand and business that informs you of every action you need to take in alignment with your highest vision.

This is the one thing that will make creating the visual aspect of your brand possible. It will inform the style of your logo, the colours you'll choose, the images and the copy you'll write that will become your brand language and look and feel.

I love the Innocent Drink story. In the late 90s, Richard Reed and two of his university friends were aware of the importance of having their "5 a day" fruit and vegetable intake but found it could be a hassle and was time-consuming to prepare. They wondered if there was an easy and enjoyable way to have the vitamin intake and decided to explore with smoothies. To test out their business idea, they had a stall at a music festival in West London, with a banner saying 'Should we give up our day job and make smoothies?' alongside a bin marked "Yes" and another marked "No".

At the end of the festival, the "Yes" bin was overflowing and the "No" bin had just three cups in it, so they decided to leave their jobs and start making smoothies full time. This is how Innocent came about.

I love this story because they noticed something they were missing themselves, and it corresponded to a need and a gap in the market for which they found a solution. I also have a soft spot for this brand from a visual point of view. Their hand-drawn logo of a smiley face with a halo perfectly communicates child-like innocence visually. It makes it approachable, and it looks "good for you". They also managed to use humour in their copy, which is a tricky thing to do as humour is so personal. It was really innovative at the time and the little bottles on the shelf always made me smile and made me feel good, just by looking at them.

Your WHY is something that's very close to your heart. When you connect with it and tune into it, you feel a sense of aliveness, increased energy and excitement and it can also make you feel quite emotional.

Clients come to me with either a strong and clear business vision, having run an established business for several years, or an instinctual business idea that they haven't yet made complete sense of which is based on a gut feeling or intuition.

The common aspect both have is the strong connection to their WHY: their vision, passion and purpose.

Here are some examples: celebrating positive achievements in schools, making sales easy for small business owners, creating paradigm shifts in human consciousness, rewriting the myth of the older woman, creating beautiful homes that enhance health and wellbeing, sharing the power of facilitation, bridging the medical world, co-creating dream homes with art.

These WHYs embody the vision and purpose of clients I have worked with who created a business in alignment with their passion.

My WHY is creating irresistible brands that capture all your senses and connect to the heart. Each time I read it or say it out loud, it reconnects me and inspires me to do the work I love.

Exercise One: Discover Your Ikigai

If you want a tool to help you define your WHY, the Ikigai model is a great structure. A concept that has long existed in Japanese culture and was popularised by Mieko Kamiya in her book *On the Meaning of Life* in the sixties, it combines key aspects of your life and what the world needs to reveal what will make you happy and have a successful life and business in the long run. What you love, what you are good at, what the world needs and what you can be paid for are the starting points.

- What you love + what the world needs becomes your MISSION.

- What you love + what you are good at becomes your PASSION.

- What you are good at + what you can be paid for becomes your PROFESSION.

- What the world needs + what you can be paid for becomes your VOCATION.

At the heart is your Ikigai, which is a Japanese concept that combines the terms "iki", meaning "alive" or "life", and "gai", meaning "benefit" or "worth". When combined, these terms mean that which gives your life worth, meaning, or purpose. Ikigai is similar to the French term "raison d'être", or "reason for being". Ikigai is that which will make you, and the world, happier.

Using your notebook, write down:

- What you LOVE

- What the world NEEDS

- What you are GOOD AT

- What you can be PAID FOR

Enjoy this exploration.

Exercise Two: Connect to your WHY

Using your notebook, take some time to write your answers
to the questions below:

- Why is it important that you bring this business idea
  into the world?

- What do you love doing?

- What problem are you here to solve?

- What lights you up and brings you joy?

- What service do you provide?

- Who is your target audience? (men/women/
  children, age group, demographics, what are their
  interests?)

- What difference do you want to make with your
  product or service?

- Who are your competitors and why?

- What sets you apart?

- Who do you aspire to be?

- What are you known for and what do you want to be known for?

- How do you leave people feeling?

- If there was one change you could create in the world with the service you provide, what would that be?

- When people look at your brand, what do you want them to think?

- How do you want them to feel?

Take time to pause, think and feel into these questions and write what comes up for you.

Your WHY is what gets you out of bed in the morning; it's the fire that burns in your heart and gives your life and work meaning.

If you want to delve deeper into your WHY, I can highly recommend Simon Sinek's book *Start With Why* which explores this theme in depth and links it to great leadership.

CHAPTER 2
What If?

'Your brand already exists in your DNA. All we need to do is unearth it and make it visible.'
Marianne Hartley

Michelangelo said he could see the completed sculpture in a raw piece of marble; all he was doing was chiselling away and removing everything that was superfluous to free it up and liberate it from the stone.

I love this analogy because it captures what happens with your brand creation too.

Your purpose, what you came here to do and your reason for being in the world is such an intrinsic part of you that we need to draw it out and free it up to make it visible. It is such a natural part of you that you may not be fully conscious of it.

The "What if?" question opens up an infinite field of possibilities that allows us to delve deeper into your WHY to connect with the essence of your brand.

What if there were no restrictions and no limits to what you could create?

What if your biggest dream could become a reality?

What if your highest outcome could materialise? What if the service you provide could create a massive shift in the world for the better?

What if your product or service could deliver something extraordinary?

What is your ultimate dream and vision?

When we set aside our restrictions and excuses and allow ourselves to dream big, connect to what we love and ask, 'What if?' with an open heart and mind, we open ourselves up to insights and inspirations we did not have before that can truly make our heart sing. Research shows that new ideas, new thoughts, new activities create new pathways in the brain that weren't present before and these have an impact on how we think, feel and act.

A client of mine was in the corporate green tech fund management world for over fifteen years, working on million-pound client portfolios. Even though he was successful and good at what he was doing, there was something missing and he was feeling a lack of fulfilment. He recently took the plunge and set up his own gardening and landscaping company.

This is what he wrote to me: 'I've completed my first garden planting design already, 68 plants over 70m^2 of beds. I chose, sourced and planted them, and included my signature Acer duo, the same that we planted on Father's

Day with my daughter. I love the fact that, as this client is on our regular maintenance round, I get to watch it grow.

The instant job satisfaction is great and I'm eagerly anticipating the ongoing satisfaction of watching the work evolve. I feel myself becoming more patient!'

Messages like these make my heart sing. I could sense his re-found enthusiasm for life as I was reading his email and it made me feel happy for him. He changed career to do something he is truly passionate about and aligned with and it is bringing him joy and satisfaction.

We often limit ourselves and give ourselves excuses for not following our deepest desires and most inspiring dreams. With justifications like not having enough time, being too young, too old, not good enough, too fat, too thin, not having enough money, not having the right circumstances, not the right degrees, not the right background... If it's not things we don't have, then the external world isn't right, economically, seasonally, geographically – the list goes on and on and you get the picture.

There is no right time to create your business. There will always be challenges. Just like the best time to plant a tree is 20 years ago and the next best time is now, the same is true for your visionary business.

I am blessed to have had an amazing business mentor, Mike Harris, the founder of Firstdirect and Egg. On our first session we explored our "What if?" and created a 100-year game. Something so big we knew we would never achieve it in this lifetime, but something so compelling that whether we succeeded or not, we would have a whale of a time bringing it into being. It was thanks to his mentoring that I launched Hartley & Soul to bring healing and design consciously together.

My 100-year game is this: What if all designs had a healing effect? What if every image and product we saw and used was a thing of beauty, lifted our spirits, made us feel good and connected us to who we truly are?

Imagine what it would be like if the people you are here to serve are naturally drawn to your business because the beautiful design of your brand acts like an energetic magnet that connects to their heart and naturally draws them to you?

This vision lights me up today as much as it did ten years ago.

I am so inspired by what Jeremy Gilley, the founder of Peace One Day created. After a successful career acting in film and television, Jeremy founded the non-profit organisation Peace One Day in 1999 to document his efforts to establish the first-ever annual day of global ceasefire and non-violence with a fixed date.

In September 2001, and as a result of Jeremy's efforts, a General Assembly resolution was unanimously adopted by UN member states, establishing 21 September as an annual day of global ceasefire and non-violence on the UN International Day of Peace – Peace Day.

To prove the day can work, Jeremy Gilley and Peace One Day ambassador Jude Law travelled to Afghanistan to spearhead a campaign that, over the years, has resulted in 4.5 million children being vaccinated against polio in hitherto unreachable areas, as a result of Peace Day agreements in the region.

Since then, Jeremy has been working to institutionalise Peace Day, 21 September across the world with Peace One Day.

Isn't this amazing?

Imagine if your brand and business could have such an impact in the world. What would yours look like?

The thought of your "What if?" should inspire and energise you and open your creative mind to fill your body with excitement and energy.

Bringing your big dream, your visionary business into the world is uncharted territory and you are creating the map with every step you take.

When I launched Hartley & Soul in 2013 to bring my two passions together – energy healing and design – I was scared I would be judged and rejected by my peers in the design community. Healing and design was a combination I'd not heard of before and launching my business was like a coming out for me, an announcement to the world that 'I am an energy healer and brand designer' and that they made complete sense to come together and didn't have to be woo-woo or airy-fairy, but practical and able to transform functioning brands into thriving ones by connecting them to the heart and soul of the founder.

One of my greatest joys is to be able to show up fully with my clients and create brands that enable them to stand out, do the work they love, shine their light and thrive.

I believe we each have something to share that is totally unique and that no one else can bring into the world in the exact same way. Creating your visionary business is your opportunity to add your unique voice, energy and beauty to the world.

Every visionary entrepreneur I know has had their fair share of struggles. One of the biggest differences between the difficulties of having a job working for someone else or going through the challenges of building your own business and legacy brand is that the struggle is part of you achieving something greater than yourself: something that you are passionate about, something that lights you up and has a positive impact on other people's lives too.

Sometimes your "What if?" can find you. As Elizabeth Gilbert says in her book *The Magic*, creativity is a muse that chooses us as an outlet.

There is a story of a professional musician who loses his work. After feeling depressed for a while and looking for something to do with his time, he decides to decorate his little girl's bicycle. She is so happy and proud of her newly-adorned bicycle that soon enough other children want to have their bikes decorated. Without him consciously planning it, this act of love for his daughter naturally turns into a new outlet for his creativity; it takes him out of his depression and brings him joy and satisfaction.

Some people think it is naïve, unreasonable or a waste of time to spend time dreaming and imagining something that doesn't exist yet. 'I'll believe it when I see it,' they might say. As with any new creation, in the creation of a new endeavour the opposite is true.

Nothing new comes into being unless we imagine it first.

Every new creation started in this way, in the unknown. Our intuition guides us when we have a strong desire to find a solution to a problem or a new way of being in the world.

Think of electricity. The lightbulb. The phone. The first car. The first plane. Computers. Smartphones.

Who could have imagined 30 years ago that we would all hold a phone in our hand and have access to the answers to any of our most weird and wonderful questions at our fingertips?

None of these existed and their inventors brought these new creations into being by asking 'What if?' and being willing to try, test, fail and try, test and fail again and again until they got the result they were after.

We are often so afraid of failure that it can prevent us from actually living our true nature and following our dreams. Being safe in our comfort zone does not equal high satisfaction. Not feeling inspired in our work translates into every area of our life. Following our purpose and finding our edge and high-performance state is where we thrive.

Everything is connected.

Who you are being in the world is in direct resonance with the people you wish to attract to work and collaborate with. When you show up in your authenticity, you attract other people who resonate with this and also wish to be the best version of their authentic selves. The beauty with authenticity is that it gives other people permission to be themselves, too.

Every successful visionary business leader will tell you that the difference between failure and success is not giving up. Virgin founder Richard Branson is one of the world's most successful and prolific entrepreneurs. He has had more failed business ideas than anyone else alive and because he never stops at failure but uses it as fuel for his next invention, he has created hugely successful businesses.

What would you be doing if *nothing* could hold you back?

What would you be doing if you could *not* fail?

To thrive as humans and in our businesses, we need to feel connected.

Disconnection leads to feelings of emptiness, isolation, depression and lack of meaning in life. No product or brand, itself disconnected from its WHY and authentic self, can fill this void.

Contribution is the antidote.

Creating your business in alignment with your highest vision and making a contribution to the world is fulfilling and nourishing. Whether you impact one person or a whole country, expressing your unique gift adds to the whole and creates unity in the world.

Contribution fills the void; consumerism feeds it.

All of us are needed. All of us have gifts. We are all here to contribute. We are all valid and valuable. From sweeping the floor to running a country, all of us are needed to contribute to the whole.

The beauty of your unique gift is needed now!

Exercise: What If? Future Scaping

Athletes train their bodies and their minds to win by visualising their desired outcome, over and over again, until it is part of the cells of their bodies. When they are not exercising physically, they train their minds and see themselves crossing the finishing line. Jumping higher than ever before. Shaving milliseconds off their best time. They see it, smell it, touch it and feel it in their mind's eye first.

The brain doesn't know the difference between what we imagine and what we experience in our day-to-day reality.

Research has shown that by imagining it first, new pathways are created in the brain that enable the thought to be more readily experienced in real life.

Take some time to daydream, write, draw or visualise your "What if?" in your notebook. Think about what you would love to do and what it would look like.

- What is your ultimate vision for your business?

- What if your business idea could impact the world in a way that no other business has done before?

- What would that look like?

- What outcome would make your heart sing?

- What one change would you love to see happen in the world thanks to your contribution?

- What turnover would delight you and allow you to live the life of your dreams?

Imagine yourself there.

- Where are you?

- What are you wearing?

- What are you saying?

- What are you doing?

- Who are you with?

- What is surrounding you?

- What are the colours, sounds, smells and textures?

- How are you feeling?

- How are people responding?

- What is changing in the world as a result?

The more detail you can give this picture, the better. Really see the images in your mind's eye and feel this in your body. Imagine yourself there in technicolour. See it like a movie.

Write key words that capture your experience. The more you can engage all your senses, the better.

Take time to write down your thoughts and connect with your "What if?" and vision regularly.

If you want to dive deeper into the creative power of the mind, I can highly recommend Joe Dispenza's *Becoming Supernatural* book, which explores the power of our thoughts in great depth.

CHAPTER 3
Who Are You Here To Serve?

'Instead of worrying about what you cannot control,
shift your energy to what you can create.'
Roy T. Bennett, The Light in the Heart

Client story

When Monika Slowikowska took over a building company from her brother, it had huge debts and was close to bankruptcy. Within the first two years, Monika managed to turn it around and make it a profitable business that was turning over a million pounds. In the third year, she was threatened with having to close down the business as another building firm in the area had been trading under the same name for a longer period of time. She was going to be taken to court and sued unless she changed the name of her company.

Monika approached me to create her new business name. We went through the brand alignment process and came up with a new name that was in true alignment with her heart and vision. What followed next amazed me.

'After renaming my business from Noble Houses to Golden Houses, my turnover went from three million to eight million within twelve months. Marianne's session helped me to align fully with myself, my values and my business, and the new name emerged from this one session alone.

'It's a totally unique process and it has helped me shift my business to be in full integrity with me so everything could flow. Now I am embodying my business fully and the image we came up with is still alive in me.

'It's as if the process helped me to connect with my soul. This translated into a sense of connectedness with my business and resulted in truly spectacular success. It almost felt like my business was a living entity and I got to connect with it.'

When you are clear on your WHY, your "raison d'être", your deep reason for doing what you do, and what you stand for, it is time to focus on who you are here to serve. Your WHY and your target audience are intrinsically linked. The best business idea is worthless unless it solves a problem for someone and makes their life easier. Every business is here to be of service to someone or something else. Knowing and being clear on the problem your target audience has and the solution you hold is key to you connecting and engaging with them.

Imagine a coin with your WHY on one side. Your audience is the other side of the coin. They are one and the same thing; complementary perspectives. Just like a coin has heads and tails, there are two different pictures on either side of your brand. Being able to describe both sides with equal clarity not only gives you a more defined picture for yourself but also enables you to communicate to others what your brand stands for and who you are here to serve.

Your service is the solution to someone's problem.

I love how James Dyson came up with the idea of creating his ground-breaking vacuum cleaner. As a young adult, James was frustrated by how difficult it was to get rid of dust in the corners of a room and how cumbersome, tricky and messy emptying a full bag of dust was. This led to the creation of his iconic bag-less vacuum cleaner and it has been a godsend for countless households around the globe. His invention came from a personal frustration. By solving his own frustration, he created a solution for millions of other people to enjoy.

As a visionary business leader and entrepreneur, it is your mission to make your dreams a reality and 'Make a dent in the universe,' as Steve Jobs famously said.

What is your dream for your life and the lives of your children?

How do you want to leave the world for future generations?

What will you be most proud of on your death bed?

In her book *On Death and Dying*, about people at the end of their lives, Elisabeth Kübler Ross says the five most common regrets people have in those final hours are:

I wish I'd had the courage to live a life true to myself, not the life others expected of me...

I wish I didn't work so hard...

I wish I'd had the courage to express my feelings...

I wish I had stayed in touch with my friends...

I wish I had let myself be happier.

This is not to depress you but rather inspire you to do what you came here to do. Life is short and we are given this opportunity to make a difference, so let's take it.

Your brand is the expression of your life's work and your opportunity to create the changes you wish to see in the world. Even if they seem a little crazy at first. No change ever came about with ideas that didn't seem crazy to begin with.

This reminds me of the John Lennon song *Imagine*. Reading through the lyrics, I'm amazed by how they resonate and how relevant they are now, just as they were then:

'Imagine all the people
Living for today

Imagine all the people
Living life in peace
A brotherhood of man

Imagine all the people
Sharing all the world

You may say I'm a dreamer
But I'm not the only one
I hope someday you'll join us
And the world will be as one'

I believe we are all connected and we need each other to co-create a sustainable world that we wish to live in and where we each have the opportunity to thrive and live to our full potential. We are stronger together, and together we can come up with solutions to the world's many challenges. When we step up, we elevate each other and inspire others to take action and do the same.

Who you are here to serve is likely to be very personal to you.

You might be passionate about helping mums going back into working life, after you experienced the challenge of this yourself.

You might be passionate about teaching 8-year-olds how to build their self-confidence, as you experienced difficulties at that young age.

You might want to create a nature reserve and protect an area of natural beauty, as your favourite woodland was cut down for a factory to be built when you were a child.

Here are some examples of the WHYs of my clients and the problem they want to solve.

Why: 'Helping entrepreneurs transform the world with powerful ideas.'
Problem: The world has challenges that need to be addressed.

Why: 'Creating paradigm shifts in human consciousness.'
Problem: The wisdom of women over 50 is a highly underused resource.

Why: 'Helping busy professionals lead a healthy lifestyle.'
Problem: Busy professionals lead stressful lives that affect their health and mental wellbeing.

Why: 'Meanings Matter: How disease is a healthy response from our body.'
Problem: Traditional medicine is limited and doesn't always go to the root of an illness.

Why: 'Bridging medical paradigms.'
Problem: Lack of understanding and misconception of Eastern and Western medical modalities.

Why: 'Co-creating beautiful homes that leave you feeling transformed, elated and delighted.'
Problem: Empty nester houses that feel soulless.

Why: 'How to fire people so they thank you.'
Problem: Managers fearing difficult conversations with their staff, which keeps them and the company stuck.

Why: 'Enabling radical perspective shifts.'
Problem: Business leaders playing safe by staying within a framework that restricts them and their employees.

Whatever your WHY, connect to it in your heart on a regular basis and feel your deep passion. Feel into the energy of your vision frequently. This will keep you motivated and determined on those odd days when the going gets tough, as it inevitably does every now and then when you run your own business. Tough times aren't an expression of failure or weakness. Tough times are a part of your business growth. Whatever size company you run, no growth happens without personal growth because you, as the founder, are at the core and intrinsically linked to the expansion and impact of your business.

Think of your current and past clients. Who do you love working with the most? What type of client makes you feel energised after having interacted with them? Which make you feel drained? Those who energise you, where work feels more like play, are your ideal clients. They are also the ones for whom the cost of your products and your fees are right.

Your legacy brand is not just about you. It is about the vision you have for the world and everyone you touch by doing what you love doing.

Exercise: Create Your Ideal Client Profile

Your unique gift is the solution to someone's problem.

Understanding your ideal client's challenges and the problem you are here to solve is key to the creation of your brand.

If you are starting up and don't have clients yet, imagine who you would most love to work with and how you want to feel, and describe them in detail.

If you have been running a business for some time, you can use one of your current clients you love working with as a basis for your ideal client profile.

Know their problem inside out. Spend time exploring it, naming it, describing it. Imagine being in their heart and mind.

Put yourself in their shoes.

What are they thinking?

What are they feeling?

What are they doing?

Be specific. The more precise you are about who you are here to serve the better as this will inform the design of your brand look and feel and all your marketing communication in future.

- What is your ideal client's lifestyle?

- What sort of work do they do?

- Where do they live?

- What hobbies do they have?

- What age group are they?

- What is their biggest challenge?

- What keeps them awake at night?

- What is missing in their life? (time, energy, money, space, confidence, trust, etc.)

Write down everything that comes to you. If you want to bring your ideal client to life even more, choose an image to symbolise them and give them a name.

And don't be fooled. Being really specific won't limit the number of clients you'll attract; quite the opposite. Being crystal clear on who you are here to serve and creating a targeted communication strategy will not only allow you to communicate to them clearly and directly, but it will also draw in anyone else outside your niche who is inspired by your ideal client description.

CHAPTER 4
What Do You Stand For?

'If you don't stand for something, you'll fall for anything.'
Alexander Hamilton

Client story

Alison Kriel had a big vision. Something she saw that was missing in her field. Having been a head teacher for several decades and having turned a failing primary school in East London into an 'Outstanding' school ranking in the top 1% of the country, she was dreaming of a space where schools, teachers and collaborators could come together and celebrate the good work they were doing and also ask for support as and when the need arose.

This vision became Above & Beyond Education and is now an online platform where schools, teachers, leaders, consultants, innovators and service providers can connect in a safe and productive space. It is about connecting professionals with a passion for education to come together and take collective responsibility for making every school a great school. Alison believes every child has a right to great education.

At the heart of Above & Beyond Education is positivity and inclusivity. This had to come through in the design of the brand, which is why the brand symbol is a colourful and vibrant overlapping ampersand, symbolising collaboration and how we are more resourceful and more powerful together.

Alison is a great advocate for positive psychology as one of the best tools for both teachers and pupils and that the more well-being teachers experience, the better they will be at teaching pupils and helping them thrive.

Daydreaming is part of you bringing the highest version of yourself and your business into being. Whatever you can imagine, you can create.

I believe your brand has the potential to be a piece of the puzzle to solve some of our world's challenges and raise the energy frequency on the planet.

Every invention and great business started by dreaming big and aiming high.

If the ultimate vision for your business venture doesn't scare you, you're not dreaming big enough. Creating something small or creating something big takes the same amount of effort and energy, so why not aim for the highest and biggest expression of your brand? Having this in place gives you a clear, more focussed and more compelling road map to implement, not just for yourself, but for everyone you will be collaborating with.

Create your brand from the inside out, not the outside in.

The design is a reflection and embodiment of you and your company's values, which is authentic, unique and beautiful and brings you joy and satisfaction. Each time you look at your brand it reconnects you to your vision, your essence and the reason why you decided to embark on this creative (and a little crazy) journey to bring this business idea into being. This *inside out* design approach is expansive, nourishing and uplifting. It doesn't just nourish you, but every person who comes into contact with it.

The Pukka Herbs brand story inspires me. Sebastian had been fascinated with plants, conservation and herbalism for many years and wanted to champion the amazing power of herbs and bring their magic into more people's lives. His big idea was to give people a delicious cup of herbal tea that symbolised everything he believed in.

Towards the end of 2001, he saw Tim's advert offering help to start-up ethical businesses. Tim had experience as a business change consultant and also had a genuine passion for the power of herbs, nutrition and therapy – and a burning desire to make a positive change in the world.

Together they decided to create a business with a big difference, where the profits served a purpose.

The name Pukka came about after some hilarious non-starters – such as 'Holy Cow'. It means 'real, authentic or genuine' in Hindi and embodies everything that Tim and Sebastian wanted their business to be; it also sounded positive and felt ripe, juicy, tasty and delicious to say.

I love the Pukka brand, the design and what it stands for. In truth, this is a design I wish I had created... It's beautiful and vibrant, simple yet compelling. The teas are delicious and each pack of tea has its unique design yet is clearly part of the same brand family. It explores new territory and answers a growing demand for conscious, organic and fairly traded products on the market. I feel very connected to the brand.

What do you and your business stand for?

What is the highest expression of your brand and business?

What is the one thing you want to be known for?

Keep on asking yourself these questions until you get to a place of inner knowing and conviction.

When we set our intention, claim our vision, put our stake in the ground and take a stand, an energetic shift happens. It is as if the planets align and situations and synchronicities appear out of nowhere that would not have taken place had we not voiced what we were going to do.

Once you know your deepest, most intimate reason for doing what you do and the highest outcome you wish to create for yourself, your business and the world, no one and nothing can shake you off balance. What you stand for is both your anchor and guiding light.

To add colour and a visual expression of what you stand for in the world, a fun, practical and powerful exercise I invite my clients to do is to create a vision board that captures the essence of their business. Clients tell me years later how transformational and invaluable this exercise was for them.

Research shows that images give us an immediate feeling. Having images that you look at on a daily basis that represent what you wish to experience is a very powerful tool that enables your dream to become a reality.

Creating a vision board of your dream and the highest vision for your business allows you to put images to thoughts, feelings and ideas. By doing that, you help ground it and turn it into something more tangible. Some of the world's most influential people agree on the power of vision boards. You have to set your intention, believe that it will become a reality and then take ACTIVE steps towards making that abstract idea come to fruition.

I remember creating my first vision board 20-odd years ago. At the time I was dreaming of having a beautiful home, a gorgeous partner and amazing clients. On my board, I had beautiful pictures of light-filled homes with lots of greenery outside the windows. I can still picture it in my mind. I have materialised the home, the partner and clients. It's an exercise I do yearly to reconnect to and expand my vision, as my life and business are always evolving and expanding.

Exercise: Create Your Vision Board

Using old magazines or images you find online on Pinterest or Google images, cut out (or save) images that make you feel inspired and have the energy of what you want to experience and create.

You can make your board specifically about one area of your life, like your business, or include your whole life: your ideal home, relationship, family, friends, lifestyle, holiday destination, beautiful scenery, etc. The sky's the limit!

Here are some ideas and directions to get you started for your business.

- The style and location of your office

- The view from your desk

- The types of people you wish to work with

- The types of projects you will be creating or collaborating on

- The impact this will have in your life and other people's lives (can be written words too)

- Objects you will have on your desk

- Your favourite pen

- Items that symbolise your achievement (a trophy, an award, someone famous congratulating you)

- The car you will be driving, or will be driven in

- Where you will dine

- Where you will go on holiday

- Where you will celebrate your success

- Where you will live

The more details you add to your board, the better. The key is for the images to make you feel good and inspired each time you look at them. If you can't find an image to represent what you want, you can also use words and quotes.

Take a few hours or an afternoon off and have fun with the process!

 I would love to see your vision boards and have therefore created the Align & Shine Facebook group, where you can post your vision and connect with fellow entrepreneurs. Join us at https://bit.ly/36y3CVK

 There's a great guide to creating vision boards on Oprah Winfrey's site. Head over to read more. https://bit.ly/3tmvJR2

PART 2: DISCOVER

ENERGY | VIBRATION | FREQUENCY
CONGRUENCE | COHERENCE

– Right Brain –

*'If you want to find the secrets of the universe, think
in terms of energy, frequency and vibration.'*
Nikola Tesla

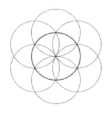

CHAPTER 5
Your Brand Frequency

Client story

Each brand alignment session is unique and an absolute joy to host. When Nikola King approached me to discuss the brand for her vision of a range of high vibrational fragrances, I was very excited and inspired. That session has stayed with me to this day. It was magic. There were synchronicities throughout the session and each time we tuned in to one of her beautiful essences another layer of magic happened. We were open to the unique frequency of her brand, and it felt divine.

This is what she says. 'There are some experiences that stay with you long after the experience itself... The brand alignment day with Marianne is one such time. Five years on, it still feels as alive and potent in my being as it did at the time. Such was the magic and the power of this work. For this reason, it is actually quite hard to put into words. I remember saying at the time: 'That is my legacy written on the walls,' and this still rings true today.

'It was an emotional experience to have my life's work brought together and formulated into an encapsulated brand – a word I find somewhat lacking, as it is so very much more than this – and for the whole time, I felt safe and seen. It's hard to describe it any other way than it was an incredibly magical experience and one I treasure deeply.

My business has taken many twists and turns since this beginning and yet the core essence of what was discovered on that day – the values, the core look and feel of the brand, the foundational messages – remain absolutely the same.'

We live in a mathematical universe and nature boasts the most beautiful designs and patterns. Whether we look at these patterns through a telescope, a microscope or the naked eye, macro and micro patterns often reflect each other. Galaxies in the sky look like the iris of a human eye. The spiral in our teacup is the same pattern as a hurricane. Planets create unique patterns with their trajectory around the sun and no two snowflakes are alike.

There is a ratio or proportion that is found everywhere in nature called the 'golden mean' or 'golden ratio', also known as the 'Fibonacci sequence' and referred to as 'sacred geometry'. The golden ratio is 1.618, as represented by the Greek letter phi. The ratios of sequential Fibonacci numbers (2/1, 3/2, 5/3, etc.) approach the golden ratio. In fact, the higher the Fibonacci number, the closer its relationship is to 1.618.

This mathematical sequence is clearly visible in a nautilus shell and our DNA molecule. The programme for all life is based on the golden section, which could explain why, when these ratios and proportions are used in art, architecture and design, everything just works and looks and feels right. It's because these measurements are in balance and harmony with our human proportions.

This ratio is also present in our day-to-day life with objects like our credit cards or our paper sizes (A3, A4, A5, A6, etc).

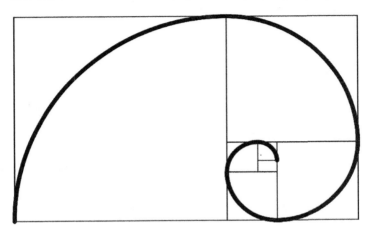

Above: A depiction of a nautilus shell and the Fibonacci sequence.

Just like the patterns present in our natural environment, your brand has its own pattern, energy and frequency. Defining how you want people to feel when they come into contact with your business identity will inform the colours, shapes, patterns, fonts, images and words to use for your brand.

Colours, shapes, words, images, sounds, scents and emotions all have an energy and frequency. Combined together, these elements are a super powerful tool to communicate your unique brand message as each builds on the other to strengthen, emphasise and enhance what you want to express.

Your brand is multi-sensory. It engages all the senses: sight, hearing, smell, taste and touch.

The movement of planets around the sun create some of the most astounding patterns. One of my favourites is the design that Venus makes on her journey around the sun, known as the 'pentagram of Venus'.

When plotted geocentrically – from an Earth-centred perspective – there is a highly noticeable rhythm in the motion of Venus. After eight years, it returns to the same place in our sky on about the same date. This is known as the eight-year cycle of Venus, and stems from the fact that

13 Venusian orbits (8 x 224.8 days) very nearly equals eight Earth years. The cycle was known to, and was of great interest to, ancient peoples such as the Maya.

The flower of life pattern I am using as part of my own brand (above) symbolises the interconnectedness of all things. It is a pattern that has been found in ancient sacred sites all around the world, from Egypt to Machu Picchu, way before there were means of communicating between these places.

Each pattern has an energy and frequency. Some are calming and some are energising. The same is true for your brand.

Colours can lift our mood or drag us down. Each colour has a different impact on how we feel and is a powerful language unto itself.

As a very broad and general guide, light colours tend to lift us up while dark colours may calm us or pull us down. The environment, proportion and juxtaposition of another colour and reason the colour is being used are key and play an important role too.

White reflects the most light and is said to hold all the colours of the spectrum, as seen when light enters a prism.

Black absorbs the most light. White, gold and silver can be used to communicate an elegant, classy and luxurious feel.

Blue and green are seen to be calming, like the sky, rivers and plants. Red and orange are associated with fire, speed and danger. In nature, the brighter and more vivid the colours are, the stronger the signal for attention.

These signals are wired into the brain and influence our emotions, which is why colours have a way of bypassing logical thought and have an instant impact on how we feel.

Colours have different meanings in different cultures. It is a good idea to check that the colours you are using for your brand do not have a negative connotation for your target audience and market.

There are some awesome books on colour; if you want to dive deeper into the subject, I can recommend *The Little*

Book of Colour by colour psychologist Karen Haller.

The shape you choose for your logo and symbol is another way to enhance and convey your message. Circular shapes tend to be more feminine and have movement in them. Square shapes tend to be more masculine and solid. The triangle is one of the most stable and solid shapes.

  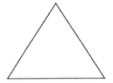

There are innumerable beautiful fonts. Serif fonts tend to give a traditional feel and represent heritage, while sans serif fonts are more contemporary.

As we know, an image tells a thousand words. Photography is another powerful and vital tool to bring your brand message to life.

The combination, composition and use of colour, shape, font and image will communicate your unique message and brand frequency.

Emotions have an energy frequency. High frequencies are love, peace, gratitude, harmony, beauty, connection and unity. Low frequencies include hate, fear, disharmony, disconnection, anger and judgement.

One way to tap into a frequency is to simply sense how what you are looking at is making you feel. If it is making you feel good, it is likely to be high frequency; if it makes you feel bad, it's more likely to be a lower frequency.

We've all had the experience of walking into a room and feeling uncomfortable, without really knowing why. And we've all had the experience of walking into a space and instantly feeling at ease. This is due to several aspects: the space itself, the proportion of the room, the design, the colours, textures, the light, the furniture, objects and their positioning, the empty space – but we can also pick up energetically on events that took place in the space in the past. Together, these elements emit a frequency and invisible energy that we unconsciously pick up on.

When you create your brand, you want to consciously make it resonate at a high frequency to achieve the highest outcome, not just for yourself but for everyone around you. By creating it in this way, your brand becomes the embodiment of this energy blueprint in physical form.

Dr David Hawkins, in his book *Power Versus Force,* speaks about the different degrees and levels of consciousness and the frequency of our emotions, with anything below 200 being low emotions and anything above 200 being higher emotional frequencies.

Low emotions	High emotions
0-20 shame	200 courage
30 guilt	250 neutrality
50 apathy	310 willingness
75 grief	350 acceptance
100 fear	400 reason
125 desire	500 love
150 anger	540 joy
175 pride	600 peace
	700-1000 enlightenment

Because there are no two people or two visions or businesses that are the same, your brand has its very own unique frequency. Being clear on what you want this frequency to be is like choosing a radio station. It will be defined through how you are showing up, what you have to offer, how you want people to feel, what you want them to think and which actions you want them to take.

As Albert Einstein says, 'Everything is energy and that's all there is to it. Match the frequency of the reality you want and you cannot help but get that reality. It can be no other way.'

Whether we are aware and conscious of it or not, we are in constant communication with our surroundings. We impact other people's energy and other people impact ours. Our surrounding impacts us too, like in an invisible conversation. Everything we see and the people and objects we surround ourselves with have an impact on how we feel.

The images we see, the people we pass on the street, the traffic, the noise, the buildings, our office, our home – everywhere we go, we are connected and communicating with what surrounds us.

Your message needs to align with who you are being so you can clearly connect with your target audience.

I'm fascinated by the doughnut economy model, which offers an alternative perspective to our current economic system. Economist Kate Raworth, who developed the theory, describes how a new financial model could address many of the worldwide challenges we face.

In her article *Meet the doughnut: the new economic model that could help end inequality,* she says: 'Instead of focusing foremost on income, 21st-century economists will seek to redistribute the sources of wealth too – especially the wealth that lies in controlling land and resources, in controlling money creation, and in owning enterprise, technology and knowledge. And instead of turning solely to the market and state for solutions, they will harness the power of the commons to make it happen.

Money creation: why endow commercial banks with the right to create money as interest-based debt, and leave them to reap the rents that flow from it? Money could alternatively be created by the state, or indeed by communities as complementary currencies: it's time to create a monetary ecosystem that can fulfil this distributive potential.'

This approach is a pattern disruptor in our current economic field and provides an alternative perspective that takes people and the earth's resources into equal consideration. It creates a very different frequency.

Defining your brand frequency will help you congruently get your message out into the world and allow others to recognise you and connect with your business.

Your brand's energetic frequency will attract the people who resonate and align with it and will have no impact on those you are not here to serve.

The clearer your frequency, the better, as it helps you and your clients identify instantaneously whether your product is right for them and if you are meant to work together or not. This energetic and emotional connection bypasses logic and happens in a fraction of a second; just like first impressions, it is subliminal.

The way you show up in life and business is all part of branding – you are an intrinsic part of your brand. From the profile picture you choose for your private Facebook account to the way you show up at networking events and respond to emails is all part of your brand. The way you show up on social media and the messages and images on your website are all part of your brand.

Being clear on the core message and energy you want to communicate before you create any marketing material will help you build a congruent message on all platforms.

Exercise: Discover Your Brand Frequency

1. Choose how you want people to feel when they see your brand.

For example: elated, empowered, inspired, fired-up, powerful, enthused, unstoppable, expanded, calm, nurtured, taken care of, pampered, connected, loved, heard, confident, in safe hands, etc.

2. If your brand was a song, which would it be?

3. If your brand was a radio station, which would it be?

4. If your brand was a movie, which would it be?

5. Choose the energy you want to communicate with your brand.

E.g., excitement, empowerment, strength, trust, certainty, love, connection, joy, gratitude, togetherness, etc.

What unique pattern will your brand frequency create?

Let your business be a pattern disruptor in your field and industry to make a positive impact in the world.

CHAPTER 6
Aligning Your Brand With Your Heart

*'The most beautiful thing we can experience is the
mysterious. It is the source of all true art and all science.
He to whom this emotion is a stranger, who can no longer
pause to wonder and stand rapt in awe, is as good as dead:
his eyes are closed.'*
Albert Einstein

Client story

Lisa Mitchell works with visionary founders, entrepreneurs
and leaders globally. She has worked with Jamie Oliver,
NET-A-PORTER and L'Oreal, to name just a few. We wanted
her brand to reflect her high energy and dynamic approach
to working with visionary founders and capture the
profound and practical changes her clients experience
through working with her. We created a vibrant colour
palette to capture the energy and a very simple, stripped
back logo that acts like a stamp to anchor the design and
embody the practical aspect of her work.

This is what Lisa says: 'I have worked with Marianne twice
now. My brand is brilliant, it is authoritative and impactful.
I've not been doing any business development because I
have clients just turn up. The brand and logo have given me
credibility, clarity and expansion.

'I feel like it embodies who I am and it's been a central solidifying factor from which everything else goes off. It has an authority and a resonance with the clients I am attracting and working with.

'We created a vision of where my business is going and I am finding that my clients are meeting me at that vision point.

'When we work together, I almost feel like I have this personal and business development, and creative process all in one go, which is really powerful. That connection Marianne has to not just me, but a bigger energetic field and bigger potential that we are both tapping into. That's the magic. I am realising more and more that alignment is the key, in everything.'

The human heart has a network of about 40,000 neurons that are comparable to those in the brain. In other words, our heart has its own intelligence.

If you were to create your brand from what you discovered in the first part of this book alone, you would already be creating a brand with depth and impact, as we did a deep dive into the WHY of your brand and dug an important part of the foundation. Connecting to the essence of your brand through the heart and soul gives us another deeper, more subtle and profound level of understanding that logic doesn't have access to. Combining both logic and intuition is where the unique power of your brand lies.

I use a simple yet profound process to get my clients and me connected to the essence of their brands and it's an exercise I absolutely love as the outcome is always surprising and totally unique. It's a short meditation that takes us into our heart and reveals words, images or feelings that inform us and connect us to the true essence and vision of the brand.

As Dr Kirren, one of my clients, said after we tuned into the heart of her brand, 'I feel like I am now energetically connected to my brand in a way that I wasn't before. I am even clearer on why I am so passionate about doing what I am doing and can feel the connection in the cells of my body.'

Innovation and breakthroughs cannot come from the known. Innovation and breakthroughs come from the intuitive mind, from the unknown.

James Dyson only employs people who are willing and not afraid to fail, lots. Why? Because innovation and breakthroughs only come from doing things that have never been done before and failure is an intrinsic part of the process of creating something new that didn't exist before.

Success is the result of not stopping at failure.

The inventor of the light bulb, Thomas Alva Edison, failed 999 times but succeeded on the 1000th attempt. Better still, he said he never failed; he simply found 999 ways of how not to do something.

When we tap into our hearts, our intuitive mind is like an infinite field of possibilities. A world where nothing exists in physical form, but the potentiality of it is already there. Just like this book that I'm currently writing – it hasn't taken full physical shape yet, but I can visualise it, feel how it's going to feel to be holding it in my hands and imagine how I'd like people to feel while they are reading it. In fact, the vision of the book is what is helping me to write it, with the end result in mind.

The heart is a higher navigation system that is connected to our consciousness, to that field of infinite possibilities, to all that is what some might call source. The logical mind is a great implementer and a great doer. Most of us spend most of our time thinking, busy in the logical side of our brain, with facts, data and past experiences. But creating outcomes that didn't exist before cannot come from old data. If we want to create something new, we need to create from the unseen and the unknown.

Buckminster Fuller says, 'You never change things by fighting the existing reality. To change something, build a new model that makes the existing model obsolete'.

Many accomplished, highly successful entrepreneurs and innovators were often not the best students in class as they spent more time looking out of the window daydreaming than learning facts. This gave them an opening into a wider, richer world of possibilities.

Creating from the known only gets as good as what has come before. Creating from the unknown is like jumping into the void and opening up a whole world of possibilities.

Both sides of the brain are vital in our day-to-day life and the best outcomes are achieved when we engage our intuitive mind to connect to further possibilities and our logical mind for implementation, making things happen in the physical world.

When your brand is connected to your heart you create an invisible link with the heart of your audience.

Exercise: Tuning Into The Heart of Your Brand

This is a short guided mediation and visualisation which is best done with another person guiding you through it. You will need your notebook and pen ready.

Sit comfortably with your feet firmly on the ground, leaning your back against your chair with your eyes closed.

Take a few deep breaths in and out of your nose and relax.

Let your body sink into the chair and relax even more.

Spend a couple of minutes breathing deeply and checking into your body to see if there are any tensions. If you notice tension, breathe into that area of your body and release it.

Acknowledge and notice your thoughts, your feelings, the sounds and smells around you, without giving them any importance. Just noticing they are there, knowing they don't matter.

Now imagine stepping into innocence, a space of mystery, in the unknown, a space where nothing exists but everything is possible.

Choose to be of service to your heart.

Imagine a beautiful circle of golden light in front of you. This beautiful circle of light embodies the vision of what your brand stands for.

Now imagine stepping into the circle of golden light and choose to receive a symbol. This can be a word, a sound, a feeling, a picture, an experience. Trust the first thing that comes to you.

When you have something, slowly open your eyes.

Start writing down everything you experienced. Whatever you saw, heard or felt, describe it and write it down. There is no right or wrong. Trust whatever you get.

It may not make any logical sense but don't worry about this; just go with it.

Let's say you got a symbol of a key.
What is obvious about it?

What texture is it? What size? What shape? What colour?

Is it an old-fashioned design or modern? Is it rusty or shiny?

What does a key symbolise for you?

Describe what else is obvious about it. Is it heavy or light? How is it used? What does the key open?
Where does it lead to?

Keep asking these questions and describe what is obvious to you. When you've exhausted the list, ask yourself how this relates to your brand.

Play with it and make it up until you feel there is nothing else to say.

Then draw out the three or four core themes that represent the heart of your symbol.

This exercise allows you to connect to the wisdom of your heart and will give you new perspectives about the essence of your brand.

I learned this technique on an intuition course lead by Darren Eden a decade ago and have been using it in my work and personal life ever since.

 If you want me to guide you through the exercise, you can watch and listen to the guided meditation here: https://bit.ly/36tQEbV

CHAPTER 7
The All-sensory Expression of Your Brand

*'A brand is a person's gut feeling about a product, service
or organisation.'*
Marty Neumeier

Client story

A huge number of entrepreneurs, business owners and
innovators want to work with a mentor, but find it extremely
hard to find one who is qualified and willing to help. Mike
Harris saw this problem and created Iconic Shift to help
people with really big game-changing ideas.

It was clear that the brand not only had to have an
outstanding and exclusive look, but also an exclusive feel to
communicate the high-level leadership training Mike was
offering to visionary entrepreneurs.

Mike built three iconic billion-pound businesses:
Firstdirect, the first telephone bank, which transformed
banking; Mercury Communications, which led the rapid
change in telecoms in the early 1990s; and Egg, the first
internet bank, which revolutionised banking again.

To represent both the depth of Mike's knowledge and the
game-changing ideas of entrepreneurs, the logo for Iconic

Shift is made up of a bold sans serif font for "Iconic", for clarity and impact, and a handwritten font for "Shift" to capture the personal transformation people experience through his mentoring programme.

The black and gold brand colours visually communicate the stature and exclusive essence of the brand. A gold foil was used for the logo on both the brochure cover and business card to create a special lift and shine. The texture of the brochure is an unusual material that has a soft velvety touch that further elevates the experience of the brand.

Mike recalls a decisive moment in a meeting. 'One senior executive had to sign off the participation of one of his teams on one of my programmes. He stroked the outside of the brochure (it's a very special tactile material), said: "If that's the quality of what you produce, I'm on board," and signed the contract without even looking inside.'

How do you influence what people experience with your brand, when a brand is a gut feeling that lives as an intangible idea in people's minds?

The value of a business lies in the brand.

Large corporate brands know that, and they look after their brand as one of their greatest assets after their employees. They make sure their mark is easily recognisable by consistently using their brand elements – their logo, colours and fonts – clearly, precisely at the same size, in the same proportion and same positioning in everything they do, at all touch points, online and offline. They know that it is only through consistency, congruency and repetition that their image will stand out in a crowded space. Mercedes has been using its logo and symbol in the same colour, the same size, in the same positioning on every single piece of marketing and advertising for decades. This consistency is what makes it possible for us to recognise the Mercedes brand within a fraction of a second, from the corner of our eye.

When your brand is an idea in your mind, it isn't yet grounded and you can be easily swayed and lose direction. But when your brand is linked to all your senses, you create a physical, embodied connection to your vision that firmly roots it and anchors it in your body.

Connecting all your senses to the brand, using sight, sound, touch, smell and taste together with your words, colours, fonts, images and texture, creates a unique all-sensory pattern that becomes your brand DNA.

Your brand DNA – this pattern that is made up of your unique combination of words and colours, colours and shapes, shapes and images, images and sounds – becomes an entity that creates an imprint that will live in people's minds, which they will come to associate with you and recognise you by.

Logo + Colour + Font + Words + Image = Brand DNA

Consistency and repetition is the key. This imprint is created by clearly and congruently using your design elements at all touch points.

To connect all our senses to the brand, we need to tap into our right brain, our intuition, the non-linear part of the brain.

The best way to do this is to treat this next exploration like a game and have some fun. There are no right or wrong answers and you cannot make mistakes.

Don't be too precious about the combination of words and responses that come up for you. Take it lightly and play with it. Don't let your head get in the way of "getting it right", but answer with the very first thought that comes into your mind.

You'll be surprised to read through your list afterwards as it will give you insights and you might see patterns or an invisible thread appear that you didn't have before. It becomes like a poem or your unique brand riddle.

I went through this exercise with Jane to explore the "taste" of her brand. When gravy came up for her, it was such a surprise that we both burst out laughing. It didn't make any logical sense, but we knew this was truly part of her unique brand signature. The connection here is the very traditional English aspect, which is in total alignment with her target audience for her personal art advisory service, The Trusted Art Guide.

You may have orange for a colour and panther for an animal and lemon for the taste. Bringing these all together gives a unique combination that only you can embody, that describes your identity to you in your own language. It doesn't mean that because orange was the colour you saw, your logo has to be that colour. But it does inform you of the feeling, the energy and the sensory expression your brand needs to have for you.

I remember the first time I did this exercise for my previous brand and business, the Jam Factory. I had cinnamon for taste and citrus for scent and simply naming the taste and scent had a profound impact on how I felt about my business. It helped me connect to it on a deeper, energetic, more embodied level.

I see a high level of disconnection in our world today and believe this to be one of the major causes of unhappiness, dissatisfaction and lack of fulfilment.

We have disconnected ourselves from nature by living in cities and buying food in boxes where the content has nothing to do with its original shape. We've disconnected ourselves from the natural rhythm of life and have forgotten that we are integral to it.

When we feel disconnected, we feel isolated, separate and alone. The world looks grey. When we are connected to ourselves, we feel a connection with others, nature and the world as a whole.

When I am connected to myself, I notice colour and beauty all around me. In turn, seeing beauty increases my connection to my heart and others; it gives me a feeling of expansion and brings me joy and satisfaction.

Your brand can be a tool for connection in your field. Consciously setting up your business from this space is your opportunity to impact your area of expertise and create a new level of connection that may have been missing before. By showing up as who you are, you inspire others to do the same.

This reminds me of Marianne Williamson's quote from *A Return to Love*, one of my favourites:

'Our deepest fear is not that we are inadequate.
Our deepest fear is that we are powerful beyond measure.
It is our light, not our darkness that most frightens us.
We ask ourselves, "Who am I to be brilliant, gorgeous, talented, fabulous?"
Actually, who are you not to be?
You are a child of God.
Your playing small does not serve the world.
There is nothing enlightened about shrinking so that other people won't feel insecure around you.
We are all meant to shine, as children do.
We were born to make manifest the glory of God that is within us.
It's not just in some of us; it's in everyone.
And as we let our own light shine, we unconsciously give other people permission to do the same.

As we are liberated from our own fear, our presence automatically liberates others.'

I believe one of our greatest gifts for being alive right now is to be able to contribute to making the world a better place, even if it is just for one other person.

By embodying your brand with all your senses, you can turn up and show up on the global stage and shine with every cell of your body.

INTENTION + EMBODIMENT = ALIGNMENT

This authentic embodiment not only increases the impact and power of your message but also connects to the heart of the audience you are here to serve who resonate with and align with your message.

Exercise: The All-sensory Expression of Your Brand

Answer all the questions with the first thought that comes into your mind.

There are no right or wrong answers. It is about engaging the intuitive side of your brain.

If you do this exercise again in a few days' time, you could get different answers.

Have fun with it!

Ask yourself this question with each of the following:

If your brand was...

> ... a colour

> ... a shape

> ... a texture

> ... a word

> ... a feeling

> ... a taste

> ... a sound

> ... a scent

> ... an animal

... a plant

... a place/location

... a country

... a city

... a building

... a car

... a watch

... a object

what would it be?

CHAPTER 8
Aligning Your Brand With Your Vision

*'Believe in your heart that you're meant to live a life full
of passion, purpose, magic and miracles.'*
Roy T. Bennett, *The Light in the Heart*

Client story

Dr Kirren Brah had been running a medical practice for several years when she approached me to refresh and reposition her brand to better encapsulate the work she does with both Western and Eastern medicine. The new design we created is distinctive and simple yet it powerfully captures the essence of two parts coming together, east and west. Her strapline "Bridging medical paradigms" emerged from the brand alignment session.

This is what Dr Kirren says: 'I came to Marianne because I wanted to redefine my brand. I had so many different ideas and was feeling overwhelmed on where to start.

Through using her special methodology, she instigated the creative process of unravelling the authentic and unique purpose of my brand.

'Marianne essentially connected both the analytical and instinctive aspects of branding in a systematic way:

1. Analytical questions that went deep into the vital aspects of my brand to help me get to the crux of exactly what my service is about.

2. Meditations that I felt accessed and helped me to articulate the subconscious vision I had for my brand.

'The process was collaborative and clearly communicated.

'Now I am working on the products for my brand, I can really see the importance and value of Marianne's work. The core features of my brand are not only encapsulated in the visual representation (logo, colour schemes, etc.) but I have a blueprint to continually build from.

'I have clarity on my brand so I can remain consistent in all aspects of my business, from how I deliver to how I market my products. I know and trust that I can retain the authenticity and values of my brand for the long haul.

'Marianne is someone who blends artistry and intuition with practical in-depth analysis to discover what she defines as the "heart and soul of your brand".'

To align your brand with your vision, start by looking at existing brands you love and asking 'Why?'

A brand I'm inspired by is The English Cream Tea.

I met Jane Malyon on a business development course called "Key Person of Influence". Jane told me how, after randomly meeting an elderly lady living locally who shared her passion for afternoon tea but could no longer travel to have her beloved treat, she: 'Literally, physically felt the lightbulb go on above my head and that truly was my Aha moment! If this lady couldn't go out to the afternoon tea... could the afternoon tea go to her?!'

After researching how many companies were already delivering afternoon tea hampers, she was surprised to find the answer was none! This was ten years ago and not only was there a gap in the market, but Jane was also surprised to be able to register englishcreamtea.com as her domain.

The packaging needed to reflect the luxurious, indulgent element of delicious afternoon tea, and it was imperative that it was also beautifully delivered intact to people's doors.

After trying out 17 (!) courier companies, even couriers transporting human organs, Jane finally found a company that ensured the treats arrived at a safe temperature and looking perfect!

Since then, her business – with a tiny team of three "scone gnomes" working in The Secret Sconery – has created its own branded range of luxury jams and over 20 fine teas. She exports to seven countries and has won Great Taste, Product and Customer Service awards.

A favourite moment came when they hosted the largest number of people gathered in one place all eating an English Cream Tea (scones, cream, jam and tea) for 25 continuous minutes and were featured in the 2013 Guinness Book of Records.

Jane says: 'As soon as I had that Aha moment, I 100% knew that this was what I was put on earth for.... and suddenly all the "dots of my life" joined together! I always wanted people to connect, to be kind and real with each other – to be considerate and truly nice. It turns out that's exactly what afternoon tea does – it brings out the best in us. Furthermore, when I was a child I wanted to be a fairy godmother when I grew up... and here I am now, sending out the loveliest treats that put smiles on people's faces. I think – by pure chance – I really did end up as the nearest equivalent to being a fairy godmother. Lucky, lucky me!

'And apparently, Nelson Mandela described afternoon tea as Britain's greatest export!'

Jane's story inspires me and makes me smile each time I hear it. I love how a chance encounter inspired her to create a business around something she is so passionate about and in full alignment with – and it is filling a gap in the market. The simple, clear and clean design of her brand beautifully captures the essence of Britishness.

Have you ever wondered why you are drawn to certain brands and not others?

We are faithful to brands we love and trust and with whose values we align.

We are surrounded by brands from the moment we get up

to the moment we go to bed. The products we use on a daily basis are branded and, whether we realise it or not, they have an impact on how we feel; they give us an experience and colour our lives.

From what we have for breakfast to what we have for dinner, from our favourite tea or coffee, our favourite bakery or coffee shop, our most loved skirt, suit or trousers, our mobile phone, our means of transport, the newspapers and magazines we read and the computer and software we use, each item is branded and accompanies us throughout our day.

Some of my clients say they aren't aware of the brands they use, but the truth is, we are all consuming brands all the time – unless we live in the midst of nature and live directly off the land – but even then, our gardening tools may well still be branded...

Are you a Microsoft or Apple Mac user?

Do you have an iPhone or Android phone? What is your means of transport? Public transport, bicycle, cab or car?

Becoming conscious of the brands you love and why you love them will inform the visual language of your brand and how you want to serve and delight your own clients.

You energetically resonate with those brands you love and are drawn to. Brands you dislike either give you a strong adverse reaction or go totally unnoticed, as they are not here to serve you. Being clear on both the ones you love and the ones you don't gives you valuable information for the creation, strategic positioning and differentiation of your own brand.

Many people buy things because of the brand. Some people purchase things because they need them, not because of the brand they are. If this is you, notice the things you purchase on a daily basis and why you do, because whether you are aware of it or not, it is a choice you make and these choices are either aligned with your values or not. If you are someone who only buys certain branded products, you will have a high awareness of the brands you love and why.

Your brand extends to every touch point your audience comes into contact with you, in the physical world and online.

Having international offices or an online shop, it is important that your customers have the same experience with you whether they are online or in London, Milan or San Francisco.

Your office, website and social media presence need to communicate the same message for people to have a seamless enjoyable experience of you, your product and your brand. When something is misaligned – for example, using a font and colour on your website and a different colour palette in your social media feed – you make it harder for your audience to build a clear and congruent picture of you in their mind and they will find it harder to trust you, without knowing why.

Imagine the experience you want people to have with you and your brand. And remember, we make up our minds within seconds, so first impressions count.

What is the first thing you want your audience to see on your website?

What do you want them to think?
How do you want them to feel?

What action do you want them to take?

How do you want people to feel when they walk into your office?

What is the first impression people have when they enter the building?

How are they being greeted?

What is the reception like?

What objects do they see first?

What are the colours, textures, pictures?

What is the lighting like?

Is there music and a scent in the hallway?

Is it corporate and business-like or laid back, warm and relaxed?

Your website and online presence is most likely where you will be making your first impact and where people will have their first experience of you. Being clear, congruent and consistent on all social media platforms is key. Give your audience a seamless and enjoyable experience so they will want to spend time with you on your website, share their delight with their friends and come back for more.

Looking at existing brands that you love helps inform the look and feel of the brand you are about to create and give an indication of the experience you want your audience to have with your company.

Exercise: Brands You Love and Align With

Designers love the Apple brand for its simplicity of the design, the elegance and the user friendliness of their products. Their packaging and range of products is distinctive and undisputedly part of the same brand family. Their minimalistic and airy shop design and layout was ground-breaking and felt more like a temple than a computer store.

Make a list of the brands that you love and resonate with and describe why.

Brands you love: Why you love them:

Brands you dislike: Why you dislike them:

If no brands are popping into your mind and you are not sure where to start, begin with the products you use on a daily basis. Think about one ingredient you couldn't do without, your all-time favourite luxury brand, or one item on your Christmas wish list.

PART 3: DEFINE

BRINGING IT ALL TOGETHER

– Joining left and right brain –

'Brand culture starts at the top.
A living brand is a set of behaviours.'
Marty Neumeier

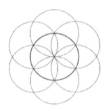

CHAPTER 9
Brand Coherence

Client story

To celebrate their 20th anniversary, the IAF (International Association of Facilitators) decided to refresh their brand to reflect their global reach, inclusive vision and high standards of facilitation. Several agencies pitched for the project and Hartley & Soul was selected.

Jeffer London says: 'The old concept was totally out of date. It was cold and grey. It had no symbolism and no heart.

'Marianne helped us figure out who we are, what we stand for and what we do.

'We realised that we are an inclusive, soft-touch, big hearted, colourful community, a fluid organisation, a network of people who choose to be part of something. The new brand and visual vocabulary she created really reflects that.

'Understanding the invisible qualities that are our values has helped us align our messages around how we tell our story and has allowed us to shine. It's not just about the colours and the font, but it is about the spirit behind it.

'So when people see the logo, it is something they identify with.

'Our facilitation standards have been accepted by governments, institutions and corporations around the world. Before, we were a small assembly based in Canada but wanting to be international. Today, we are a truly international association in 70 countries.'

You have dived deep into the heart of your brand, dug the foundations, discovered what is unique about you and your offerings, who you are here to serve and the difference you want to make in the world. Now it's time to bring it all together, to plant the seeds in the ground and draw up the building you set out to build.

This section is about joining logic and intuition, joining the left and right brain, making your brand coherent and putting your stake in the ground.

Brand coherence is achieved when every aspect of a brand is aligned. When the visible and tangible aspects truly reflect the invisible and intangible.

The intention with which we create the brand also plays an important part in the design. Holding the highest intention, impact and outcome we wish to have with our business while creating the visual aspect of our mark energetically embeds it in the design; it becomes part of the energetic fabric of your brand and is an aspect of what I call a healing design.

Aligning our brand with our heart's yearning allows us to step out into the world as a whole integrated being, not just as a part of ourselves. We can show up fully and shine. It is more joyful, and our clients receive a more authentic and fulfilling experience from us. It's a win-win situation.

This heart and soul connection makes our life more enjoyable as we show up in more fullness and every interaction is more meaningful. It creates ease and flow, more creativity, more freedom, more fun, more expansion because we are not trying to be something or someone we are not. Living from this place of possibilities and living in alignment with the highest expression of ourselves is an expansive and contagious energy.

This magnetises your ideal clients to you and attracts your ideal employees, who resonate with your highest vision and want to play their part in it.

I believe each one of us is a piece of a puzzle. We each have an impact on the whole. Together, we can find solutions to solve the problems we face when we hold the vision of a united world, where everyone has a voice and everyone has the opportunity to live their best life and thrive while making a contribution.

When we play our part in alignment with our vision and values, it is like a finely-tuned instrument playing in harmony.

Having a beautiful brand that is aligned with your heart and soul gives you confidence, certainty and pride to show up fully.

If you imagine your brand as a building, your vision, mission and values are the invisible structures that will ensure your business is firmly grounded. They are the spine of your business, the most important components of your brand, your core navigation and your North Star. The logo and design of your brand is the exterior façade of the building, the visible aspects of your brand, that need to reflect and communicate what you stand for.

Your vision is your purpose, your ultimate goal and your WHY. It is the drive and motivation that gets you out of bed in the morning. Your vision needs to be so inspiring to you that simply thinking about it makes you smile and spring into action. You want your vision to stretch you to its ultimate expression beyond where you are and take you out of your comfort zone.

Your mission is the journey to make your vision a reality. It's the actions and steps you will take to go from where you are now to where you want to be. It is your unique formula for making your vision a reality.

Your values are who you are being. They're the attitude and attributes you have at the core of your brand to make your vision a reality.

I'm inspired by 4ocean's vision. Alex Schulze and Andrew Cooper created 4ocean after taking a surf trip to Bali, Indonesia, in 2015 and seeing the amount of plastic present in the sea. They decided to build a company that would employ local fishermen and boat captains to remove plastic from the ocean and envisioned a business model where the materials 4ocean crews recovered from the ocean would be used to develop new and innovative products that raise awareness about the ocean plastic crisis, fund a global ocean cleanup operation, and empower individuals around the world to end their reliance on single-use plastic.

Their vision is to see a thriving ocean and healthy planet.

Their mission is to end the ocean plastic crisis.

Their values are sustainability, re-usability and awareness.

Defining your vision, your mission and your values is your brand's energy blueprint. It forms your brand's most important words. They hold the highest frequency of you and your brand and will guide you every step of the way in building and growing your business. Any action you take, be it writing copy for your website, writing a news article, email or social media post, the key words you have chosen for your vision, mission and values need to be present and infused within the text you write.

This will create a clear and congruent message by which your audience will recognise you and ensure a consistent tone of voice.

Using this as a navigational blueprint to guide each and every action and inform you of your next steps ensures you remain aligned with your WHY and quickly shows you if you are going off track, as the words won't resonate.

Creating a name for your new business, a product or strapline needs to have your brand frequency embedded within it. Use the questions and exercises laid out in this book to define your brand's unique energetic blueprint.

Aim for a short simple name as it is more memorable.

The visual aspect of your brand needs to reflect and embody your inner values through the words, images and colours you use.

Exercise: Define Your Vision, Mission and Values

Distilling your vision, mission and values into three adjectives will help create a base for your brand to grow from. By defining these, you have the core ingredients for all your marketing material. Every social media post, newsletter, article, advert or website copy emerges from this. They are your brand DNA and the key words you will come back to over and over again to check that what you are creating is aligned.

    —   Choose three key words for your vision.

    —   Choose three key words for your mission.

    —   Choose three key words for your values.

Here's an example from one of my clients:

Vision:	Mission:	Values:
1. Freedom	1. Connect	1. Sustainability
2. Expansion	2. Recalibrate	2. Conscious co-creation
3. Joy	3. Integrate	3. Truth

CHAPTER 10
Your Brand Promise

'Business shapes the world. It is capable of changing society in almost any way you can imagine.'
Dame Anita Roddick, Founder, The Body Shop

Client story

Shelley Whitehead approached me to refresh her brand as her business offering was changing. Her branding no longer worked or reflected the deep transformational work she was doing and the people she was working with.

Shelley says: 'You can get a graphic designer to knock up a logo, but when someone works with you, it is quite different. What I got from working with Marianne is a structured, professional approach where she was fully present to me, and the essence of what I am about. The process was then translated into a congruent look and feel that has enabled me to grow with a very clear message to attract the clients I want to work with and for them to really value what we do.

'Most people starting out in business aren't aware of what branding is, the true cost of branding and the real value of it.

'What people discover through the process is the essence of their brand and the essence of them.

'It's like making a whiskey. Then you have a fine whiskey that has been distilled over time. There's a distillation process to Marianne's branding methodology.

'The new brand is much more contained and serious without losing that essence of transformation and blooming that my clients experience. It has had a huge impact on my turnover.

'When one feels congruent and you're very proud of your design because this is who you are, you just step into it. When we have the perfect fit with our brand, we just feel really confident and everything else blossoms from there.'

Your brand promise is about delivering the experience your service claims to your audience. It is about building trust. By showing up consistently with clarity and congruency, your audience can recognise you, engage with you and love you.

Clarity + Congruency + Consistency = Brand Promise

One way to build trust with your audience is to share your story. Everyone has a story to tell and there are no two stories that are the same.

As a visionary business leader you are at the heart of your brand, and your path and life experience colour the expression of your work, whether you are running a lifestyle business or a multinational. Your personal story is a central point and core element of your brand and one of the jewels of your business.

The path you have been on that led you to create your business is totally unique and an enticing piece that can be used in a multitude of ways to connect, engage and build trust with your audience. And we all love a good story!

I'm still inspired by what Anita Roddick, the founder of The Body Shop, created in the late seventies. She pioneered social change through her belief in something revolutionary: that business could be a force for good.

When The Body Shop first opened its doors in 1976, it was a little green-painted shop in the streets of Brighton, England. Its approach to beauty was radically different to the big players in the beauty industry. It was simple – ethically sourced and naturally-based ingredients from around the world, in no-nonsense packaging you could easily refill. Products and beauty rituals made for every body, that made women feel good in their skin – never promising to make them look like someone else.

Over 40 years ago, this kind of approach was ahead of the curve. With Anita's passion for the planet and campaigning for causes, The Body Shop was always more than just a beauty brand. It had purpose – profit and principles working in harmony. The products were never tested on animals and didn't exploit anyone in their production. They worked fairly with farmers and suppliers, and helped communities thrive through their Community Fair Trade programme. Today, there are more and more brands following in their footsteps, and they're glad to welcome them aboard. The world needs it.

Anita Roddick believed that beauty was a person's source of joy, comfort and self-esteem. It was what you liked about yourself, and what made you feel good. Her beauty products, she believed, were more about a daily ritual of self-love instead of the false promising of slimming and anti-ageing that the industry pedalled. She didn't want to create products to make women look a certain way, but to help them be the best versions of themselves.

Anita was an activist at heart. It's what gave The Body Shop its unique purpose and drive for social change. A true feminist and human rights activist, she built the brand on empowering women and girls with every product and every business decision, striving for equality and creating opportunities for women through their Community Fair Trade programme. Principles some labelled as "feminine" – inclusivity, collaboration and compassion – are the foundation of the brand. She said: 'I think all business practices would improve immeasurably if they were guided by "feminine" principles.'

Imagine if your brand could have an impact like this in a sector that is close to your heart. What would it be? What would you be transforming, revolutionising or creating?

How would you tell the story?

Share your personal story and your passion with your audience. But be sure to check that each and every post carries your brand values. If it doesn't, don't post it. Always share with the perspective of 'Will this add value to my audience?' Sharing what you have cooked for dinner is a must for a chef. It may not be so relevant for a leadership coach.

Your brand is as unique as your fingerprint and your brand story is one of the lines.

Exercise: Part 1: Define Your Brand Story

Make a list of key events that have taken place in your life, the decisions they created or impact they had on you, and your reason for bringing your business to life.

Some of us have had several businesses and you may be running more than one business at present.

Making a list of all the stages in your life will give you an overview to help you reveal your unique brand story. Patterns and connections will arise that you were not aware of before.

Here are some pointers to get you started. Feel free to add to this list as it is not exhaustible.

- Where you were born

- Environment

- Political situation

- Major events at that time

- Childhood

- Parents

- Siblings

- Grandparents

- Friends

- Pre-school / school

- Games you loved to play

- Pets

- Favourite foods

- Something you hated

- A challenge or a shock

- Travel

- Education

- Higher education

- Charity work

- First job where you received money for doing something for someone else

- Key events – positive and negative – that had an impact on you

You can look at your life in chunks and draw out key events in this way:

0 – 7 years

7 – 14 years

14 – 21 years

21 – 28 years

Etc.

Working with a copywriter can help you draw out the essence and key points of your story and distil it into an enticing piece. This can feature on your website and provides content for various marketing pieces that will make you stand out authentically.

Exercise: Part 2: Create Your Strapline

A great way to communicate your brand promise is through your strapline. A good strapline is short and snappy. The shorter the better. My strapline is 'Creating irresistible brands'.

Reading through what you have written for your WHY, your "What if", what you want to be known for, your vision and values, create a short sentence that lights you up each time you say it. A powerful short sentence has the ability to reconnect you to your vision each time you share it with someone, whether you are meeting them in a lift, a train or at a networking event. It's the sort of phrase that you feel in your whole body and it makes you feel connected and alive.

What you want to be known for + How you leave people feeling = Winning structure for a strapline

This is a golden nugget to use in your pitch to encapsulate your brand DNA.

CHAPTER 11
Your Brand Presence

'If your actions inspire others to dream more, learn more, do more and become more, you are a leader.'
John Quincy Adams

Client story

Herman Stewart saw a real need for children to be mentored in schools, and not just the children with the best or worst grades, but every child – and especially those who go unnoticed because they are neither great nor bad but don't stand out because they don't make much noise.

'My brand has helped clients, partners and supporters to understand what we do by sharing our ethos within the brand. My turnover has grown, and my work has grown in credibility and impact amongst clients and peers. My mentoring is now recognised globally as a leading brand.'

Your brand presence is made up of all the elements that build connections with your audience. You can think of it like a garden that you need to tend to regularly so it can grow and flourish and the weeds don't creep in...

Your brand elements are:

- Your name

- Your logo

- Your strapline

- Your brand colours

- Your fonts

- Your image style

The value of your business lies in you being able to protect the name and the logo of your brand. The first thing you need to do with your new business is to register the name.

Work with an IP lawyer to trademark your brand name. Trademarking your business name before embarking on the design of your logo is key to ensuring no one else is trading under the same name in your industry. Make a selection of 3-6 names that can be checked for availability, protectability and stand-out. It is particularly important if you intend to grow your business internationally. Having to change your business name after trading for some time is not only costly financially, but can also cost you the reputation you have built up with your brand. Having to change name and/or logo means having to rebrand and rebuild your reputation to regain your customers' trust in a new brand.

The trademarking process can take several months depending on your industry, so allow time for this in your business schedule.

Once your brand name is trademarked, you can proceed to create your logo. You will find guidelines on how to brief a designer in the next chapter.

The following are things you need to do to successfully take your brand out into the world. Commissioning an expert in each area will save you time, heartache and resources in the long run and help you thrive.

- IP (trademarking your brand name and logo)

- Design (logo, website)

- Photography (personal headshots and core brand images)

- Copywriting (engaging written content that has your tone of voice)

- Marketing (positioning your business to reach the audience you are here to serve)

- PR (your brand and story being featured in newspapers and magazines)

- Social media (Instagram, LinkedIn, FB, Twitter, TikTok, Google, YouTube)

- Video (short videos of you sharing your pitch or a new product)

- Advertising (online and offline)

Your brand is about establishing TRUST for your customer and BELIEF in your product everywhere your customers come into contact with you.

Visibility + Credibility + Consistency = Lovability

Visibility is where you show up and where people can find you, online and in person.

Credibility is the expertise you bring and the problem you solve for your audience and the experience you have built in your field.

Consistency is having a congruent message using your brand elements and showing up regularly to make it easy for your audience to recognise you.

Lovability is the result of visibility, credibility and consistency combined and how seamlessly your audience can connect, engage and fall in love with your brand to become raving fans.

Your brand is particularly present and visible online.

With every message you post, think about:

- Engaging your audience

- Adding value

- Showing that you have a solution to their problem

- Giving answers to the questions they have in their mind

- Having a clear call to action (follow us on Instagram, connect on LinkedIn, sign up to our newsletter, book a call, buy our latest product, join us at next our event, etc.)

Define where you want to establish your presence online and in the physical world.

Create a variety of posts and balance between:

- Sharing inspiration

- Sharing someone else's content that relates to your target audience

- Showcasing your expertise

- Sharing a personal post

- Selling a product

- Sharing a client testimonial

Have your key audience in mind and always aim to add value rather than focusing on selling your product or service.

Your website is one of your most important components for establishing your brand presence. Use your logo and brand colours consistently throughout your website. Make your copy easily digestible. Think of the user and make it a pleasant, easy-to-navigate, enjoyable and intuitive experience.

Keep the design and the information clear and not too busy.

Make your key messages stand out and have small amounts of text below, unless it is a research or technical website where you need to add a lot of detailed information. In all other cases, less really is more. Bear in mind that writing less takes more time as you have to simplify and distil the information you want to communicate to the essence of what you want to say.

The functionality of your website needs to reflect what you offer, what you want people to receive, the actions you want them to take and what they are going to get in return.

Being passionate about what you do is key to running a successful business that is aligned with your values.

When you do what you love and love what you do, new situations and opportunities open up to you.

- Your business flows when you flow

- Know what makes your heart sing and do as much of this as you possibly can. Outsource the rest

- Build a team with people who have complementary strengths and talents to yours

- Choose people who share your vision and values to work with so you are all singing from the same hymn sheet

- As you grow, your business grows. When you stall, your business stalls.

Keep an eye on your vision at every step of the way and check that your next action is aligned with it. If it is not, change or revise the action.

Over the page is an overview of where your brand appears and how to keep all the elements consistent so you stand out and make it easy for your audience to recognise you and connect with you.

BRAND PRESENCE

Website

Advertising

Social Media

ONLINE

Newsletter

Email marketing

Podcast

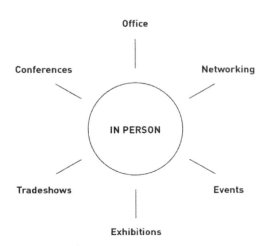

Office

Conferences

Networking

IN PERSON

Tradeshows

Events

Exhibitions

Know where your target audience spend their time and tailor your communication accordingly to best connect with them.

When your images, colours and messages are aligned with you and your highest intention for what you are here to do, it resonates with the people who you are here to serve.

When your message is right and your price is aligned and you communicate it clearly, your target audience will respond to it and you will be oversubscribed. You will either have to turn clients down or create a waiting list and let people know you will be free to work with them in three or six months' time.

BRAND SUCCESS WHEEL

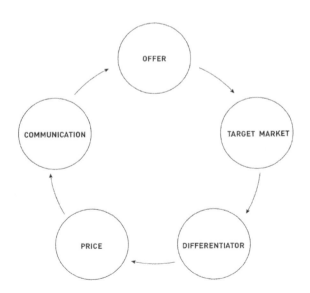

You then have a choice whether you want to set up a team and grow your business or run a lifestyle business and have a waiting list of clients who want to work with you.

Daniel Priestley talks about this in his book *Oversubscribed*, which I can highly recommend.

You will find that the principles you use to create your legacy brand are the same for living a fulfilling life, in alignment and resonance with your true essence.

Exercise: Define your brand presence

Your brand presence is created by how and where you show up as a person, how you showcase your products and services, and the platforms where the world can find out about them.

Make a list of your products and services.

You will likely have a core product or service and several sub offerings.

- Your core product and service is:

- Your sub offerings are:

Here's a list to get you thinking of places where you want to be visible.

Online platforms

LinkedIn   Facebook
Twitter   TikTok
Instagram   Google
YouTube

Print

Newspapers: local, national and international
Magazines: trade, specialised, financial, special interest

Events

Networking
Speaking
Conferences
Trade shows
Podcasts
Peer groups

Office or shop

Your physical location

Choose where you are going to be active and how often you are going to show up and share with your audience: once or twice a day; once, twice or three times a week; monthly, etc. The right amount will be what works best for you and the people you want to connect with and serve.

CHAPTER 12
Bringing Your Brand to Life

'Don't be pushed around by the fears in your mind.
Be led by the dreams in your heart.'
Roy T. Bennett, *The Light in the Heart*

Client story

Wendy Yorke left the corporate world behind to follow her passion and set up her own business helping people to write, edit and publish their books. She approached me to redesign her website.

Wendy says: 'To start with, I struggled with the emphasis you placed on the intention you and I put into the creation of my website. I didn't understand the importance of why you needed to go into that depth to be able to design a website. I didn't get what it would do for me and how investing in doing it right would make it work so successfully.

'It was a big step for me at the time but now, five years on, I can say it has done all the things I wanted it to do. You designed a website that would work for me in the long run, not just for right now. It has helped me bring in the clients I want to work with. To me, that is the success of the design.

'I get really great feedback about my website. What I love about it most is that a lot of people say that when they looked at my website, they knew I had a deeper message than all the other agents they had looked at. And that's what works for me. What I love is that they see something in my website design that they feel, without the words being written.

'I think it's all about energy.

'My mission on the planet right now is to help other people to write, edit and publish their books, to spread their message to help others. I love that they get the message, without reading the words.

'The way you create a brand and the design of a website energetically holds where you are moving to in the next 5-10 years. There's the intention first, then you create the design to encapsulate the message of the intention.

'Clarity needed to shine out of my website – and it does.'

The visual representation of your brand is like the tip of an iceberg, and accounts for 20% of your brand. It needs to powerfully and succinctly express the 80% of your brand that is the invisible aspects you have discovered throughout this book.

Successfully translating your essence into the visual expression of your brand happens from the inside out.

Now that you know the invisible elements that make up your brand foundation and you're clear on what is at the heart of what you do, you are ready to brief a design agency or designer who will bring your brand to life visually, ready for the world to see.

Two things I would highly advise you do. First, you must love the work they have produced for previous clients and feel aligned with their values, and second, you must like their personality.

Have an initial meeting, ask questions and see how you feel. See if you can imagine spending a few hours a week or month with this person or team over the next three, six, twelve months, depending on your project.

The creation of your name, logo, strapline and website is a co-creative process. Choosing a designer or design agency with whom you have a good connection will make your collaboration a joy, as you will spend significant time together bringing your brand identity to life.

Follow your gut instinct. Someone might look good on paper and come highly recommended, but that doesn't necessarily mean it will work for you.

Once you know you have found the person or agency you wish to work with, define how you are going to work together. The clearer you are on the outcome you want to achieve, the better the result will be. Designers love being given a clear brief and then space and freedom to create and bring their creative solutions to you.

Share the brands you love and the look and feel you want your new brand to have.

Is your brand more a VW camper van or an Aston Martin? Is it bold, classy, elegant, authoritative, fun, established, innovative, cutting edge, ground breaking, timeless?

Be clear in your brief but not too prescriptive. For example, don't say: 'I would like a blue heron on top of the first letter of the logo in red serif type,' as this is not where creativity flows... But you could say: 'I'd like a heron, because this bird symbolises X, Y and Z for me, and I'd like it to be associated with the letters of the brand name,' for example.

It is a balance between being clear on the outcome you wish to achieve and giving the designer freedom to explore and come up with a creative solution that you will not have thought of, that goes beyond what you could have imagined. Let yourself be surprised and delighted; that is what you commission a creative agency for.

Having a structure in place will ensure you have a smooth and enjoyable journey together. Three things you must agree on before you start are:

- Time frame

- Outputs and deliverables

- Budget

I have come across disillusioned business owners who received a design for a logo or website they didn't love, and in some instances they felt they couldn't tell the designer.

This breaks my heart. I can see this happening for two avoidable reasons: one, the designer didn't ask enough questions and created something *they* thought worked around the idea they had of the client, rather than something that worked *for* the client; or two, the brief was unclear and too loose, which left it open to misinterpretation.

This can be avoided by having an agreed set of action steps in place, so each person knows what needs to happen by when and with whom and removes false expectations.

- Start with the end in mind.

- Discuss how many rounds of design there will be. Will you be shown one, two or three designs and have two rounds of refinements?

- Define how often you will be communicating with each other – daily, weekly, monthly.

- Map out the full project with key milestones.

- Agree on the sign-off process.

- Know how many people have a final say on the design. (Hint: the fewer, the better.) If a group or team is involved in having the final say, make sure everyone is informed of the timeframe and process so you can keep to the timeline.

- Put key deadlines in place to ensure you have all the necessary items ready for your launch. Add a little breathing space for anything unexpected that may crop up.

- Know what success looks like for you and communicate this with your designer.

- Ask them what success looks like for them too as this will ensure you are aligned.

- Finally, and most importantly, enjoy the process!

Your brand creation is the most important piece of your business success, besides your employees. Your brand will support you and assist you in sharing your message and will be a key part of what makes your business valuable and sellable, should you decide to sell it at any point.

If you ever think about selling your business, your trademarked brand will make it much easier. This is where your assets lie.

The design of your brand is the exterior of the building you have imagined – the walls, windows, doors and roof; the materials and textures of the house.

It is the field you have ploughed and seeded, ready to be harvested.

It is bringing the values of your brand to life.

How to brief a designer check list

To create a comprehensible brief for a designer, summarise all the outcomes of the exercises in this book. Here is a quick overview:

1. Your vision, mission and values

2. What you do

3. Who you do it for

4. What you stand for

5. How you want people to feel when they interact with your brand

6. The brands you love and dislike and why

7. The look and feel of your brand

Write up a contract

Agree on

    –   Time frame

    –   Outputs and deliverables

    –   Budget

Do

— Agree on how you are going to work together.

— Agree on milestones and deadlines.

— Agree on the number of meetings you will have.

— Agree on deliverables (logo, brand guidelines, website, exhibition banners, social media profile, social media posts, adverts, etc.).

— Give the designer a clear brief.

— Tell the designer the outcome you wish to achieve.

— How you want to feel when you look at your brand.

— The brands you love and why.

— The styles you love and why.

— Who your ideal clients are and how you want them to feel.

— What action you want your clients to take, having seen your product or service.

— Give the designer creative freedom.

— Ask questions if anything isn't clear. There are no silly questions.

Don't

— Be too prescriptive.

— Tell the designer how and what to design.

— Micro-manage.

— Make assumptions. If anything is unclear, ask for an explanation.

Having a clear roadmap will put everyone at ease and lead you to a successful outcome. A good relationship will make working with your designer and agency much more enjoyable and reap better results.

Enjoy this unfolding.

IN CLOSING

There were many moments of resistance once I chose to write this book, and many days of not feeling aligned. As soon as we decide to put something out into the world, we get to experience the opposite of that, too. As if to be fully qualified to write about a subject, we need to experience the absence of it first, to get a better understanding and have a truer picture.

There were moments of doubt and the one thing that brought me back to writing each time was the knowledge that I was writing for myself first and foremost. This book has been in my heart and soul for a long time and it was fascinating to watch my resistance come up each time I wanted to sit down and write. It seems the closer something is to our heart, the greater the resistance. Can you relate?

This book is part of my WHY, what makes my heart sing. Showing up fully to work with visionary business leaders is pure joy and revealing the beauty of their business through their brand feels like magic. I am blessed to work with clients who are open to dive deep, claim their unique space and put their stake in the ground.

So each day I chose to write, not because I had to, but because I wanted to - for the sheer joy of it!

This resistance made me realise another thing – that many of my clients come to me when they are feeling stuck and are unsure or have no idea of how to bring their vision into being. They have gone through their own version of resistance before coming to me. Going through this myself gives me another level of understanding of where my clients are at and what they may have been going through before reaching out to me.

Resistance shows up when we are about to bring something new into the world and there's a fear of what might happen if a) it fails or b) it is successful. In either case, we know we won't be the same person that we were before, as the process we will have gone through will have transformed us. It's the fear or the unknown. Our ego wants to keep us safe. Our ego means well; it wants to make sure we do not get hurt or repeat a challenging experience we may have had in the past – but it has no imagination. The danger here is to listen to the resistance and not take action!

When an inspired idea comes to us, it is also our opportunity and responsibility to act on it and make it come about. Our heart and soul know there is more for us to experience in our life and there is this longing for a world we know is possible, even though we are not yet seeing it or experiencing it in the outside world. Our heart-felt longing knows the truth of what is possible in every aspect of our lives and the invitation to follow this longing is there, but as this means stepping out of our comfort zone into the unknown, it can be terrifying.

The unknown is a field of possibilities of pure creative energy, where every thought and idea already exists as a potentiality. Your new business idea already exists in this field; we just have to unearth it and give it a name and a shape.

It is such a joy to work in this energetic field and allow a new brand to emerge from there. It is one of the most beautiful and satisfying experiences to have with clients and is often very moving, too. When we connect with the uniqueness and the deepest drive for the creation of the business, there is tangible magic in the room, and there are usually tears of joy. This moment is transformative and visceral; it is like giving birth to a new idea and the idea being seen and acknowledged fully for the first time.

We are facing many challenges that are directly linked to the survival of all life on the planet. Choices we make on a daily basis have a global impact – where we buy our food and clothes, where they were grown or manufactured, how far they had to travel to reach our plate or our closet. Our choices either support the renewal of our planet or harm it. We can choose to be part of the problem or become part of the solution.

My wish is for this book to play its part in protecting and sustaining this beautiful planet, which is why I am actively taking part in the UN Sustainability Goals by supporting Goals 14 and 15 and donating 10% of every book sold to www.4ocean.com and www.coolearth.com.

THE GLOBAL GOALS
For Sustainable Development

RESOURCES

Reading

Start with Why – Simon Sinek

The Magic – Elizabeth Gilbert

Becoming Supernatural – Joe Dispenza

The Little Book of Colour – Karen Haller

Power Versus Force – Dr. David Hawkins

Oversubscribed – Daniel Priestley

To Listen To

Doughnut Economy – Kate Raworth

Visionary Founders – Lisa Mitchell

Client Brands and Websites

www.hartleyandsoul.com/alignandshine

ABOUT THE AUTHOR

Marianne Hartley founded Hartley & Soul branding and design agency in 2013 to bring together two of her passions, energy healing and design.

With over 25 years in design, she has worked with some of the world's largest brands, from the Queen's Diamond Jubilee Pageant, Intercontinental Hotels, Toyota, Bacardi, Bonhams Auctioneers, The Royal Academy of Arts and Taylor Woodrow to the pharmaceutical and not-for-profit sectors, start-ups and visionary business leaders.

Having met many talented business owners with brands that didn't communicate who they were and what they did, Marianne decided to put her methodology into a book to be used as a guide to create the solid foundation for a long-lasting and impactful brand, whether a person was just starting up or creating their tenth successful business.

Marianne's passion for beauty in nature and art since childhood has led her to believe that beauty has a healing effect that can be encapsulated in a brand. Deep enquiry into the heart and soul reveals the hidden beauty of a business and the design is the energetic blueprint or DNA of the brand.

Connect

LinkedIn: Marianne Hartley

Insta: @hartleyandsoul

Facebook: @hartleyandsoul

YouTube: @HartleyandSoulBranding

Website: www.hartleyandsoul.com

ACKNOWLEDGEMENTS

It is said that it takes a village to raise a child. In many ways it has felt the same with the writing and birthing of this book. So many people played a part in its coming to life, and I am touched and deeply grateful to each and every one.

To my husband Philippe Fleury, for supporting me and encouraging me to write throughout and for believing in me in the moments I didn't.

To my mother, Denyse Borel, for instilling her love of life, art and beauty in me and for being such a constant positive force and guiding light in my life.

To all my clients, for entrusting me with their vision and for the beautiful co-creative collaborations.

To Mike Harris for being an incredible mentor and vision holder with me.

To Daniel Priestley for the KPI programme, which was a total game changer for my business.

To Marty Neumeir and Andy Starr for creating the brilliant Level C programme and community of branders.

To Ellen Watts, my book coach extraordinaire, for her guidance and support and holding the vision for the book with me.

To Sue Ingram, for her ongoing support, wisdom and priceless input.

To all the beta readers – Sara Maxwell, Natasha Wardle, Dr Kirren Brah, Ansal Trafford and Alison Kriel – for being the first to cast their eyes on the manuscript and provide valuable feedback.

To Brittany Read for supporting me and cheering me on to the finishing line.

To Noemi Savoldelli for her invaluable input at the final stage of the book.

To all the inspiring business owners, teachers, visionaries, coaches, mentors and collaborators I have had the pleasure of meeting and being inspired by throughout the years.

To my amazing friends for their love and care and for being part of my life's journey.

Thank you all from the bottom of my heart for playing your part in making this book a reality. I am deeply grateful.

May this book be a spark that lights the fire in your heart
and inspires you to do what you have always wanted.